Common Bushes Afire with God

Kieran M. Kay, O.F.M.Conv.

*To the Poor Clare Sisters
in Canton, Ohio
in deep gratitude
for pointing the way
to Francis and Clare*

Grateful acknowledgment is made to *The Apostolate of Our Lady* to reproduce essays contained in these pages.

First published in 1994 by Resurrection Press, Ltd.
P.O. Box 248
Williston Park, NY 11596

Copyright © 1994 by Kieran M. Kay

ISBN 1-878718-23-1
Library of Congress Catalog Card Number: 94-66743

All rights reserved. No part of this book may be reproduced or transmitted in any form or by any means, electronic or mechanical, including photocopying, recording, or by any information storage and retrieval system without permission in writing from the publisher.

Cover design by John Murello
Illustrations by Sister Joan Marie Jones, P.C.P.A.

Printed in the United States of America.

Contents

Foreword by Adrian van Kaam	9
Preface	11

Winter

1. Waiting for Life	15
2. Let It Be	17
3. The Word Is Heard in Silence	19
4. Choose Life	21
5. The Gift of Christmas	23
6. Epiphany	25
7. That We May Be One	27
8. Headaches and Heartaches	29
9. Longing to Belong	31
10. Christians and Cults	33
11. Truth and Customs	35
12. Beyond Appearances	37
13. Of Blindness	39

Spring

14.	New Life	43
15.	The Power of Powerlessness	45
16.	Words from the Cross	47
17.	Eastering	49
18.	Down the Up Staircase	51
19.	Compassion Brings Life	53
20.	Sounds of Silence	55
21.	Prisoners of the Lord	57
22.	Take Off Your Shoes	59
23.	Leaving the Garbage Behind	61
24.	Roofing	63
25.	The Roar of Pentecost	65
26.	Releasing the Spirit	67

Summer

27.	Fountain of Life	71
28.	Getting It Together	73
29.	Where Is Your Heart?	75
30.	Prayer Napping	77
31.	Addicted to Jesus	79
32.	We Are Pilgrims	81

Contents

33. Transformation	83
34. We Die without Poets	85
35. The Ordinary Touch of Divinity	87
36. Passion for Truth	89
37. Treasures of the Church	91
38. Count Your Blessings	93
39. Balance	95

Autumn

40. The New Jerusalem	99
41. Intimacy	101
42. Clowning in Cincinnati	103
43. A Temple for God	105
44. All That Glitters	107
45. What's in a Fad?	109
46. To Be a Saint	111
47. Wells for Others	113
48. Sacred Relationships	115
49. The Resurgence of Women	117
50. The Gift of Depression	119
51. Stillness	121
52. A King Forever	123

Foreword

This book is like a little shrine of light and joy in the midst of our lives of fuss and flutter. A shrine built with the shiny stones of clear and simple words. They sing about the beautiful things in our everyday existence. To our own peril we are wont to pass them by carelessly. Every time we enter this shrine, through any of its fifty-two doors of short striking meditations, we are reminded of our forgetfulness.

This shrine of words is filled with the spirit of Jesus; it breathes the joyous mood of two of his special friends, Francis and Clare. How much we need the ballads of the hearts of these two troubadours of love divine. How hungry we are for their message in an age in which many hearts are growing cold, infecting us too often with their own frostiness. You will find the Franciscan spark and lucidity everywhere in Father Kieran's lofty essays that cannot leave your soul untouched.

No matter where you dive into this little book, you will be surprised by flowers of wisdom that will light up your day. Take the last lines of Father's poem, "Let It Be."

> *Peace is my gift to you*
> *today and tomorrow and forever*
> *a peace as simple and still*
> *as water touched by the sun,*
> *as dew on the face of this lovely rose*
> *that opens at your feet —*
> *just for you.*

He could not have portrayed better the intent of this work. Every one of his meditations will open up for you some little rose that blossoms at your all too hasty feet. Instead of stepping on it carelessly, you will treasure it as a precious reminder that life is not that colorless after all.

How well Father Kieran knows that his treasures of wisdom can only be reminders if we receive them with a mind that has become silent. Silently passing through the portals of his words, we may enter the Word in and behind the words of all writers who let themselves be inspired by Jesus. It is in that spirit that Father Kieran ends one of his winter meditations with a quote of Catherine Doherty:

> Silence is more powerful than any words except one; the Word. It is by entering the Word that to some the gift of utter silence, and therefore complete speech, is given.

I am sure that we cannot better thank the author for his beautiful contribution to the sources for our everyday spiritual life than by silently entering the Word that he loves so dearly.

The more we do so, the more in the words of Kieran, "We come to adore Jesus the Christ. We know that the original Epiphany was only the first revelation of Jesus to the world. Every day there is a new epiphany, a new theophany. We need to be alert and ready, living in our peace-center in the silence of a listening heart.

"While teachers can point us to knowledge, theologians to religion, and philosophers to reason, God points us to Jesus. For all that we need and all that we can yet be are found in him."

May you and I be blessed by the Epiphany of Jesus in every page of this wonderful book.

ADRIAN VAN KAAM, C.S.Sp., PH.D.
June 24, 1994

Preface

THERE'S A LITTLE POEM by Elizabeth Barrett Browning that has spoken profoundly to me over the years. It goes like this:

> Earth's crammed with heaven,
> And every common bush afire with God.
> Those who see take off their shoes,
> The rest sit round it and pluck blackberries.

This little book is about the common bushes, the everyday things of life that most of us, most of the time, pass by or think nothing of because we are so pathetically busy. It's an attempt to allow those common things to speak to us about our loving and gracious God. Making connections between the common bushes and the fire that we call God is what our life is all about. It is what makes life exciting, an adventure, an inner journey into God. Seeing God in the common bushes lights up our life with joy in the way that God intends it to be.

There are fifty-two reflections (or spiritual editorials, as I like to call them) here. They roughly follow the liturgical seasons, beginning with Advent and ending with the Feast of Christ the King. The reflections need not be taken in order, however, since they do not follow the Scripture readings for each week and are not developmental. They are more seasonal in the sense that they follow the order of nature. Perhaps they could better be seen as following the seasons of the heart.

My heart, that is. But since my heart and yours are fundamentally the same, I'm hoping that our hearts will be awakened to the same things.

May I suggest that you savor one reflection slowly at the beginning of the week. Allow it to sit inside you for the week. Review it occasionally during the week and see how it relates to you, and how it checks out with your experience of life as it unfolds during the course of the week.

I pray that this book will bring you some of the joy in reading it that it has brought me in writing it.

Feast of the Stigmata of St. Francis
September 17, 1993

~ 1 ~

Waiting for Life

ADVENT is my favorite season of the year. It speaks so powerfully to me of the need for learning how to wait well.

We live in a culture that is directly opposed to watching life unfold in its own time. Everything is instant; every desire must be instantly gratified. This is the price we pay in a consumerist, thing-oriented, everything-now society like ours.

My parents were patient people, sensing as they did that waiting for things until their time was a value that carried over into the spiritual side of life. We were not poor, but they felt that it was important for my sisters and me to learn that we *earn* our toys by doing our family chores faithfully. And to learn that we have just one toy at a time, and get the most of it. I still remember the one toy that my parents got me for Christmas when I was about six: a Tinkertoy. Dad had constructed an airplane out of it, complete with a motor that ran the propeller. I was so excited when I saw it on Christmas morning that I ran toward it and couldn't stop, with the result that I knocked over the Christmas tree. I felt terrible about that, but my parents seemed to understand my enthusiasm and I was forgiven. Waiting for that Christmas gift, and others in other times, was somehow all tied up with the meaning of Christmas. I slowly learned that.

As time went on and my configuration of life developed, I saw how waiting entered into all of life. I saw that there was a time for everything and that nothing could or should be rushed, without suffering some sort of violence that was built into the nature of things.

I saw that the seasons of the year had their own important messages in their own time. I saw that waiting entered intimately into the birth of Jesus at precisely the right point in human history. Slowly, I began to sense my own appearance on the human scene as planned by God for a long, long time. Eventually, I began to see that I had to wait for the right words to say at the right time, for the right people to appear at the right time, for the right thing to do at the right time. I began to see that waiting was at the root of the connectedness of all of life. That's the way God planned it all; and to upset those plans results in boredom, chaos, violence.

Sadly, the world is filled with bored people who think that life is meant to be pleasurable and entertaining at all times; if it is not, then they will resort to some sort of violence to bring it about. We have to re-learn how to wait patiently for life to unfold as it is meant to in *God's* plan. Perhaps the best time to do that is Advent.

"The Lord delights in those who revere him, in those who wait for his love" (Ps 147).

> ~ *I saw how waiting entered into all of life. I saw that there was a time for everything and that nothing could or should be rushed, without suffering some sort of violence that was built into the nature of things.*

~ 2 ~

Let It Be

In the midst
of the joy of life,
I find myself lingering
on the words of Isaiah:
The flowers of the field
blossom in the morning
and wilt in the evening;
but the word of the Lord lives on forever.

I have noticed lately
more of the wilting
and less of the blossoming
more of the dying,
and less of the rising.
That's where I am at this point on my journey of faith.

It is a comfort to me
in the midst of the fleetingness of life,
as flowers and friends wither away,
to hear again the resounding echo of Jesus:
I tell you all this
that in Me you may find peace and life;
abundant life that will never end.

Be rooted in Me
at all times and in all places
and emerge from the corners of the night.
Take My hand
and each other's hands;
stand in a circle of love,

and shout the victory song together:
Death shall have no dominion.
Let not your hearts be afraid;
courage swallows cowering and mellows suffering.
Peace is my gift to you
today and tomorrow and forever
a peace as simple and still
as water touched by the sun,
as dew on the face of this lovely rose
that opens at your feet —
just for you.

~ 3 ~

The Word Is Heard in Silence

I SIT IN THE SILENCE of my reading room. On the chair next to me sits Fuzzy, my beautiful koala bear, in silence. Opposite us sit — in silence — Hugs and Huggles, the wonderful stuffed dogs someone gave me last Christmas. Fuzzy and Hugs and Huggles are powerful reminders of what the undercurrent of my life must always be, the permanent stance that I must take as life unfolds before me. I especially need that reminder as we again enter Advent.

There's something marvelous about Advent. It carries with it the excitement that Mary must have experienced as she carried Jesus within her that first Advent. I like to think that Mary spent a great deal of time dreaming about the future of her Child, still in the womb: what He would look like, what He would say, what He would do. She must have caressed Him countless times, as she indulged her maternal instinct in playful reverie. Those had to be ecstatic moments.

I can't imagine Mary in those precious moments before the birth of Jesus except as held in the deepest kind of silence. There is a time for silence; and surely one of those times, as every mother worthy of the name knows, is the whole birthing process and experience. It is too profound for words. It is indescribable. It can only be understood in the silence of the heart.

Advent calls us all to silence again. Not because it's a nice thing to do, but because it's a necessary thing to do. It's the only way that the Word can take on our flesh, and it's the only way that we can enflesh the Word. Christmas means nothing if it is limited to the sentimental songs and tinsel of a world apart from Jesus. There is no real celebration apart from our bringing Him to birth in our hearts and letting Him reign there. Catherine Doherty puts this succinctly:

> Silence is more powerful than any words except one: the Word. It is by entering the Word that to some the gift of utter silence, and therefore complete speech, is given.

~ *Advent calls us all to silence again. Not because it's a nice thing to do, but because it's a necessary thing to do. It's the only way that the Word can take on our flesh, and it's the only way that we can enflesh the Word. Christmas means nothing if it is limited to the sentimental songs and tinsel of a world apart from Jesus.*

~ *4* ~

Choose Life

The year is quickly coming to a close. Everyday on the radio we are reminded how many days we have struck off the calendar, and how many days we have left in the year. I suppose, to some, this is a valuable piece of information.

It is not valuable to me. It suggests to me that time is a commodity; that each day is no different from any other day; and that the anticipation of the next day, the next week, the next month, the next season is greater than the reality that is coming. Withal, it seems to me like indulging in a cheapening pipe dream. And it blinds us to the treasure, waiting to be discovered, that each day is; and to the gift, totally undeserved, that each day brings.

To be more concerned about how many shopping days are left before Christmas than about the significance of Christmas itself is a sad commentary on our value-system. That unfortunately is a reality in most peoples' lives, even on those who proclaim themselves to be followers of Christ.

We can turn that around. We can do that by choosing to live each day fully in and with the Lord. He, then, becomes the focus of each day: he makes every moment special, every word significant, every act a stepping-stone into deeper life. Our life then becomes the adventure that it is meant to be.

Mary teaches us that as we make our way through Advent. She teaches us to treasure the present moment as God's gift; to turn over in our hearts and find the significance of each day's events; to say yes to the God who has come, who will come again at the end of time, and who is coming each day;

to savor silence as the entry to meaning; to be overwhelmed by the graciousness of a God who wants to enter fully into the human scene.

It will do little good to erect our cribs if we do not give birth to Christ in the world. We dare not miss our chance to be the mother of Jesus by extending his Kingdom. Here. Now.

> ~ *Mary teaches us to treasure the present moment as God's gift; to turn over in our hearts and find the significance of each day's events; to say yes to the God who has come, who will come again at the end of time, and who is coming each day; to savor silence as the entry to meaning; to be overwhelmed by the graciousness of a God who wants to enter fully into the human scene.*
>
> *It will do little good to erect our cribs if we do not give birth to Christ in the world.*

~ 5 ~

The Gift of Christmas

I PONDER THE SCENE in 2 Samuel, 7–8. It speaks powerfully to me of what Christmas — and all of life — are meant to be.

King David is settled nicely in his cedar palace, feeling like the king he is, when suddenly it occurs to him that there is a glaring incongruity in his life: he lives in a magnificent palace, and the ark of God dwells in a flimsy tent. The prophet Nathan is privy to David's concern. The Lord speaks to Nathan that night, telling him to relay to David this message: You want to build a house for me? Forget it, David, I'm very happy with this tent, it allows me to pull up stakes and be with my people wherever, in their wanderings, they go. No, *I want to build a house for you*.

God was of course faithful to his promise. He set up a "house" for David and his descendants — a house and a kingdom that would endure forever; a throne that would stand firm forever. Finally, from that house that the Lord would build, would come the Anointed of God, the long-awaited Messiah, Jesus the Savior. The final tent that would house the Savior would be the womb of Mary of Nazareth. She would cradle him within her for nine months and would at last give him to the world in the fullness of time. He would appear in the flesh — a human being, like us in every way except sin (Phil 2). He would be the image of the invisible God (Col 1) because he would in fact be the Son of the Most High God, born from the heart of the Father before all ages, before whom all the nations on earth would bow in adoration. "And the Word became flesh and made his dwelling (pitched his tent) among us, and we saw his glory, the glory of the Father's only Son, full of grace and truth" (Jn 1:14).

We can get so preoccupied with building a house for God and proving our love for him that we become prisoners of ourselves. We cannot see beyond our noses. We want to be able to say to God: "I am worthy of your love. I have earned it." It's not that what we do is wrong. We surely do all those nice things out of some semblance of love. But we have forgotten that *God has first loved us;* and because of his love, we are lovable and capable of loving. We must learn the hard lesson that all that we are and have and can do is gift. We can do *nothing* to deserve God's love. All we can do is open our hearts to receive the gift of love. And even that is God's doing.

Christmas is a time, then, not primarily for giving gifts, but for receiving the Gift of Life. The Father has not reached into his gift-bag and doled out mementoes of his love; he has given us the gift of himself in the person of his Son. He has not given us a candle to light; he has given us the Light of the world. We know that with our heads, but that truth has not fully made its long journey to the heart. Otherwise, how do we account for all the futile and demonic ways that we selfishly try to prove our love for God?

Christmas is a time to receive the Gift of God. Once we have learned how to receive Jesus — in quiet, in peace, lost in wonder and praise at the goodness of God — then we are in a position to return love. Not for any reward, not for proving anything to anybody, not even for eternal life, but solely because of the demands of love. Then our focus will be clear and right; and we will be caught up and held in God's goodness, not imprisoned in our self-righteousness. "In this is love: not that we have loved God, but that he has loved us and sent his Son as expiation for our sins" (1 Jn 4:10).

~ *We must learn the hard lesson that all that we are and have and can do is gift.*

~ 6 ~

Epiphany

Even as Christmas still lingers in our consciousness, overwhelming us with the mystery of God taking human flesh without ceasing to be God, we slide quickly into the epiphany of God, the showing of this God to the whole world.

The Eastern Church calls this, more properly perhaps, the Theophany, the appearance of God in human flesh. "Here is our Enlightenment," says Robert Pelton, "our perfect light. Here is the one light which is both wholly human and wholly divine. Here is the one light which is not reason only, but also Love; not faith only, but also flesh; not hope only, but also experience; not only heaven opened, but earth reborn. Here is the one light which enlightens not merely the just and the bold and the holy, but the poor and the sinner as well. Here is the Enlightenment so splendid that it brings a silence deep enough for humankind to speak to God with God's own Word."

Our world is shrouded in a darkness so deep and so pervasive that we crouch in fear, knowing that the end is near. Death speaks more realistically to us these days than life. We huddle together in megamalls and stadiums, in bars and courtrooms — anywhere that we can feel the comfort of other human beings, friend or foe. We bolt our doors and gaze through our windows at the flow of death outside. We tremble inside.

We need to re-learn the fundamental truth that we cannot build our houses on sand. We cannot build on fear. The winds of evil are too strong. They will tear us apart. We need to build on rock. And the only rock that can withstand the terrors of the night is Jesus. He has come to set us free from the crippling paralysis of fear.

"You need not fear," he tells us again and again. "You must stand firm and believe that I have overcome the world and its deceits. I am the Way and the Truth and the Life. Outside of Me there are only shadows and lies and debilitating detours. Let go of all the ways that you are clinging to trifles that thrive today and are gone tomorrow. Let Me flood your heart with light that can turn all your fears into a holy boldness that the powers of hell cannot withstand. Let go of all your power plays to control life. The only power that you must seek is the power to surrender and the power to serve and love and proclaim Me as Lord. Let the fire of my love burn away all that is not of Me in your heart. Desire only Me, and all will be yours. Put away your playthings and find your joy in Me. Be the child that you can be with my grace — full of trust, full of wonder, full of hope, full of love. Be simple. Be content with only what you need to live life fully — only what satisfies your heart. Be at peace with yourself; let Me be the source of your peace. Do not look over your shoulder at what others have; do not lust for their possessions. And do not compete with others for status and recognition and honor. Lose yourself in Me, and let Me be your treasure. I am with you always; I am in you always. And I am enough."

We come to adore Jesus the Christ. We know that the original Epiphany was only the first revelation of Jesus to the world. Every day there is a new epiphany, a new theophany. We need to be alert and ready, living in our peace-center in the silence of a listening heart.

While teachers can point us to knowledge, doctors to medicine, theologians to religion, philosophers to reason, God points us to Jesus. For all that we need and all that we can yet be are found in him.

~ *Every day there is a new epiphany, a new theophany.*

~ 7 ~

That We May Be One

JESUS PRAYED, before he went to his death, that we may be one even as he and the Father are one (Jn 17:11). What kind of unity is Jesus praying for? That we may look alike, dress alike, talk alike?

Just the opposite is the case: we are one, we are uniquely ourselves, when all that is distinctly ours has been activated. Then alone are we in a position to give glory to God.

All of us long for unity on just about every level of life: physical, emotional, intellectual. People who do not experience unity with others feel alienated and marginalized. They do not feel at home with themselves, and consequently with others, which is one of the most painful experiences of life. As a result, they run away from life and take refuge in alcohol, drugs, sex — anything to soften the harsh reality of life.

Only a comparatively few have the wisdom to understand the kind of unity that Jesus prayed for. And we know that since *Jesus* prayed, it is within our possibility to achieve that unity, at least to some degree.

Jesus knew that his every step was guided by the Father; his heart was one with the Father's heart. He knew on any given occasion of life what he was to say, what he was to do. To do the will of the Father consumed him. He and the Father were one.

That is the same oneness that we are invited to. For that, we must "put on the Lord Jesus Christ," as Paul says. We must have the same mind as Christ. We must be open to the

Father to let his word be heard. And we must act in faith on that word.

That brings unity. That brings peace, security, clarity of vision, purpose, fulfillment, ecstatic intimacy with God.

~ *We are one, we are uniquely ourselves, when all that is distinctly ours has been activated. Then alone are we in a position to give glory to God.*

~ 8 ~

Headaches and Heartaches

IN THE DEAD OF WINTER — which is often our season of discontentment — we begin to experience a lot of heartaches. For some, the heartaches are due to being cooped up indoors. For others, they derive from dismal, dark days and precious little light from a seemingly unfriendly sun. For others yet, the possibility of encroaching death begins to wind its tentacles around them. Whatever the cause, heartaches can be nasty. And the cause is almost always deeper than what we immediately perceive.

There's a big difference between headaches and heartaches. To get rid of headaches, we simply take some aspirin. That doesn't remedy the source of the headache, but it does ease the symptom: we no longer look cross-eyed at reality; we feel like living again and can, we say, deal with the cause of the headache at some other time, which time of course never comes. We simply get on with our life and numb ourselves with distractions until the next headache comes, and then we repeat the process.

Heartaches can be somewhat similar in origin, but are different in other ways. They are not usually lessened by pills, though an anti-depressant can help on occasion. What heartaches are mostly about is the common longing that all of us are consumed by but find it difficult to articulate: the longing to be filled with infinity, the longing to penetrate beyond space and time into the eternal. In short, the longing for God, who alone can satisfy the human heart.

Heartaches can lead to fuller life or deeper death, depending on how we approach them and treat them. They can lead to fuller life if we accept them and let them speak to us about what we need to learn from them. They can lead to deeper death if we ignore them and drown them out with distractions that keep us on the periphery of life, which is the entrance to the graveyard. In that case, we have unwittingly chosen death long before our obituary appears in the local newspapers.

James Thurber once said: "All people should learn before they die what they are running from, and to, and why."

Try that on for size. It may be a key that can open your eyes as to why you have had so many heartaches recently — the thousand natural shocks that, as Shakespeare reminds us, "all flesh is heir to."

> ~ *"All people should learn before they die what they are running from, and to, and why."*
> —James Thurber

~ 9 ~

Longing to Belong

In the midst of the winter we look around us and see the signs of why we feel the way we do: the trees stripped of leaves, the grass browned from the hardening cold, the snow piled high in the parking lots of plazas. The cold has chilled our hearts, too. We feel the pain of separation from the earth: it does not open its arms to us and invite us to lie in its embrace. Most of all, we feel so far from one another at times.

There is a deep longing in every human heart to belong, to be accepted, to be part of the human scene. We long to feel connected with others, to be linked with them in some way, at least superficially. The desire for intimacy with a few wants to be stretched into intimacy with many. If that desire is blocked long enough and completely enough, we begin to harbor violent thoughts about people, and those violent thoughts can easily erupt in violent actions to ourselves or others. We begin to strike out at those who ignore us, even those whose friendship has meant so much to us in the past.

All of this because we are not at one with ourselves. We are fragmented inside and are not accepting the human condition as it touches us personally. When the signs of separation begin to appear, we need to go apart and allow ourselves the luxury of the tears of healing. We need to be put together again.

Nothing puts us together again better and applies the glue at the right places than the thought (based on the reality of God's word) that we are strangers and aliens no longer. We are fellow citizens of the household of God (cf. Eph 2:19–22). We are God's children. We belong. And belonging is what life is all about.

We are important, all of us. No matter how small our gifts, our responsibility to be all we can be is terrifying. God has *chosen* to need us. Unless we are *living* stones in the building that God is erecting, all of us are going to suffer. We do not gain from another's loss, nor do we lose from another's gain. We gain or we lose together. That is God's plan.

The choice is ours: we can drift apart in an uncaring way and suffer the pain of abysmal gaps between us; or we can recognize God's gift of belonging to him and therefore to each other, and respond lovingly.

Again, the choice is ours.

~ *We are God's children. We belong. And belonging is what life is all about.*

~ 10 ~

Christians and Cults

RICHARD HARRIS ONCE SAID, "There are too many saviors on my cross." There is, in fact, only one Savior, Jesus the Christ. All the other so-called messiahs since then have come and gone. They made their pitch, attracted people who in their insecurity ran after them, and then faded away. Only Jesus remains because only he was sent by the Father to save us from our futile and meaningless way of life.

Because of the abundance of cults these days, it is well for us to be alert. It is necessary for us to be able to distinguish the true from the false prophet. One of the most basic ingredients of the true prophet is that they *always* point to Jesus as the one sent by God. The false prophet will *always* point to him/herself as being bigger than life itself. John the Baptist will stand forever as the model of the true prophet: "He (Jesus) must increase, I must decrease." Jesus must be exalted and glorified as the one and only Savior.

The leader of a cult is interested only in self-glorification and will tickle our ears with all kinds of new phrases and half-truths that sound good, but do not agree with the revealed word of God and lead only to self-exaltation. We can so easily be misled by them because we are always vulnerable to hero-worship, especially in shaky times like ours.

On the other hand, a Christian needs to be aware of their call by baptism to be a prophet, as Jesus was prophet. That means that we all need to be mindful of our responsibility as disciples of Christ to proclaim the word of God by all we say and do. We need to proclaim the word of God openly and boldly so that the Word can take flesh within us, as the Word took flesh in Mary, Queen of Prophets. She spent all of her life giving Jesus to a hostile world, and for that she suffered. Simeon's prophecy that her heart would be pierced with the sword of contradiction was fulfilled.

So it will be with all authentic prophets. With their quiet peace-center, they will listen to God's word and allow it to sink into every pore of their being. Only then will they be in a position to speak that word with power, for they will be one with Jesus. "I live, now not I, but Christ lives in me," Paul said.

The power of that word evokes a challenge to a world asleep in mediocrity and complacency. That word, therefore, will always be hated by the vast majority of people who are adrift in the worship of pleasure, power, and self-exaltation. But the poor in spirit will hear — those for whom Jesus is truly the way, the truth, and the life — and they will continue to be the true prophets of a Kingdom that will last forever.

> ~ *So it will be with all authentic prophets. With their quiet peace-center, they will listen to God's word and allow it to sink into every pore of their being.*

~ 11 ~

Truth and Customs

I'LL BET YOU'VE NEVER HEARD of St. Turibius of Mongrovejo (1538–1606). His name is so strange that you want to turn away from him immediately. So did I until I read something that he said which knocked my socks off.

Turibius was born in Spain and educated in law. Later he taught law at the famous University of Salamanca. So brilliantly did he teach that he was asked to fill the vacancy of the archbishopric in Lima, Peru. But, he argued, he was *only* a layman. No problem! He was ordained a priest, then a bishop; and off he went to Peru, arriving in Lima in 1581, at the age of 43.

Turibius worked zealously to carry out the reforms mandated by the Council of Trent. He was especially tireless in attacking injustices and in caring for the poor. A story is told that on one occasion when he was opposed in his reform efforts by an adversary's appeal to tradition, he replied: "Christ said, 'I am the truth'; he did not say, 'I am the custom!'" Off flew my socks!

Now that's a mouthful. How many of us have tried to justify our behavior on the basis of tradition? Now that's not necessarily a bad argument. It could, in fact, be a very forceful argument at times. After all, where would the Church be without its long tradition to support its positions? But what we're talking about here is appealing to tradition when it is not revelatory of the *truth*. Then it becomes just a matter of, "But we've always done it that way!"

All of us develop traditions in our behavior. We usually refer to them as *habits* — doing the same things over and over in exactly the same way without any mental exertion. And of course that's all right. It certainly saves time when time is of the essence. If we didn't have those habits, it would take us forever to do things that should ordinarily be taken care of without any time for reflection.

But sometimes we need to stand back and take a look at those things that we do non-reflectively. We need to see if, in the light of the truth as we now see it, we might *better* do what we have to do. Truth does not change, but our *perception* of the truth changes as we enter a new level of understanding it.

We need, then, to be circumspect. We need to keep our eyes on Jesus at all times. We need to ponder the Gospel every day to see how Jesus, who is the Truth, handled everyday life. The Pharisees, for example, were not bad people; they were just in such deep ruts that they were unwilling to consider the possibility of having to change their views. Jesus attempted to shift their security from permanence to truth. He failed of course. And so the Pharisees remained in their blindness. They refused to budge, refused to acknowledge the possibility that there might be a better and truer way of seeing and doing things. That was their sin, and they remained in it.

In these days of accelerated change on just about every level of life (including, and perhaps especially, the ecclesial level), we need Turibius and his kind of divine wisdom to teach us the relative value of things. That comes only when we take the time for quiet and develop a peace center out of which can emerge the truth. Keeping our ear to the ground and responding lovingly to the Spirit as he speaks to us is the only way for a disciple of Jesus to live. That's the only option in love. The alternative is the unfreedom of untruth.

~ *Keeping our ear to the ground and responding lovingly to the Spirit as he speaks to us is the only way for a disciple of Jesus to live.*

~ 12 ~

Beyond Appearances

It strikes me from time to time (and recently more than ever) that as I watch the parade of life, I see people concerned more about preserving an image than about pursuing the truth. This contributes enormously to the mayhem in which we find ourselves.

The net result for people in this condition is blindness to anything that bears a resemblance to truth. Blindness to the purpose in life, to a sense of meaningful values, to any grasp of an inner journey. The most pitiable thing about this kind of blindness is that those who travel this road know nothing of their blindness. Everything, they tell themselves, is just fine. Just keep up the appearances. Save the surface, as the old paint company said, and you save all.

As long as people are content with this mind-set, they will continue to spin their wheels and go nowhere. They are destined to drifting through life, with all kinds of defenses to assure both themselves and others that the image is still intact.

Sooner or later this whole contrivance of illusions will have to break down if people are to see the light. As they experience swallowing their words, they sense something is wrong. There is a hollowness inside that begs to be attended to. That is the moment of truth — the challenge to put aside the nonsense and accept the reality of their blindness; or to be so overwhelmed with the reality of untruth that they must cover up at all costs and go on with the sham.

Jesus alone can set us free from this insanity. He is the way, the truth, and the life. To live in the Way which Jesus is, is to live with eyes wide open to the truth about ourselves and about the world, to live so deeply in Him that we become immediately aware of any subterfuge that we are tempted to hide behind. The truth, then, will set us free to be real, to accept the limitations that are within us and all around us, and to live within them. We begin to understand that humility is essential to real life, that our creatureliness is not a liability but an asset. We begin to understand that we are asked to be nothing but ourselves and that holiness lies therein. All the ego defenses must fall away one by one until we are left naked and vulnerable and defenseless. As we lose ourselves in Jesus, we begin to find ourselves. The true self begins to emerge, and we can taste freedom at last.

This is what Jesus was trying to teach the Pharisees; and this is what he continues to teach all who are so preoccupied with their own righteousness that they are no longer capable of seeing reality. "I came into this world for judgment, so that those who do not see might see, and those who do see might become blind." Some of the Pharisees who were with him heard this and said to him, "Surely we are not also blind, are we?" Jesus said to them, "If you were blind, you would have no sin; but now you are saying, 'We see,' so your sin remains" (Jn 9:39–41).

Jesus calls us not to try to live up to an image of ourselves, but to be a child of God made in his image. That is the way into truth and freedom. That is a loving response to God our Father that leads to clarity of vision. Blessed indeed are the clean of heart, for they will see God.

~ *As we lose ourselves in Jesus, we begin to find ourselves. The true self begins to emerge, and we can taste freedom at last.*

~ 13 ~

Of Blindness

OUR BLINDNESS IS SO PERVASIVE that it will take a global healing to bring us into the light and onto the path of sanity. Ironically, as we grow more sophisticated in the area of scientific investigation and discovery, we seem to regress in the area of what constitutes wholeness in life.

There are two kinds of blindness: physical and spiritual. The former blocks out the beauty of creation to us; the latter destroys the balance of creation. Of the two, spiritual blindness is of course worse and more serious by far. "It is only with the heart that one sees rightly. What is essential is invisible to the eyes." So said the Little Prince. He was remarkably correct.

Spiritual blindness means that we no longer recognize the invisible world as infinitely more important than the visible world. When that happens to us, we have lost our balance in life; we have lost our vision of what is important and valuable; we have lost our way. Only our openness to a stroke of enlightenment, a bolt of God's light can redeem us. Otherwise, the quest for meaning in life dies. We become slaves to gadgetry, unable to see beyond what is visible to the eyes.

Jesus is the healer of all blindness. He is the good shepherd, leading us into truth and life. He is the way to the Father, a light for our path and a lamp for our feet. Only by losing ourselves in him will we be able to find ourselves. That is his promise, and only those who surrender to him experience the fulfillment of that promise.

To be physically blind is no sin. Jesus made that clear as he healed the man born blind (cf. Jn 9). What *is* a sin, Jesus says, is to say that we see when in fact we are spiritually blind; when in fact there is no truth in us.

Jesus is the light of the world. In him there is no darkness. Those who walk in his light know nothing of inner darkness, even if for some reason they are plunged into exterior darkness. "All that came to be had life in him and that life was the light of men, a light that shines in the dark, a light that darkness could not overpower" (Jn 1).

~ *"It is only with the heart that one sees rightly. What is essential is invisible to the eyes."*

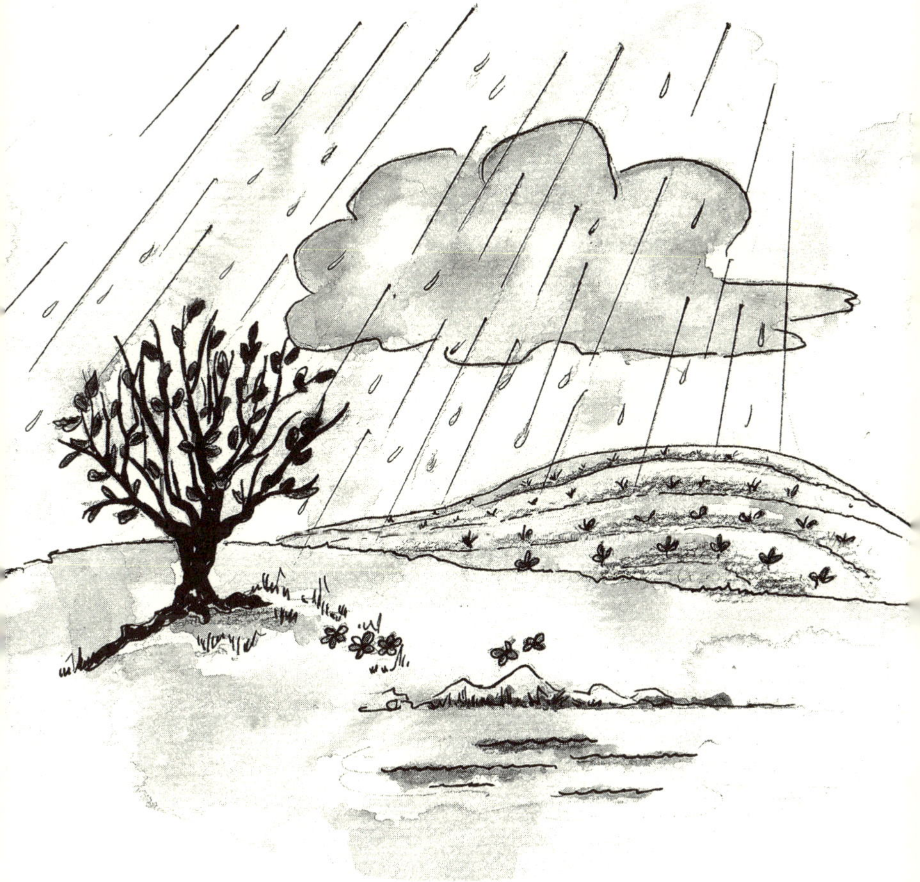

~ 14 ~

New Life

There are signs of spring all around us: the greening of the land is a reflection of the more important greening that is going on within us. There is new hope, new life; there are new dreams. The dark, threatening days are becoming less frequent; the searching sunlight beckons us to contemplative wonder at the beauty of all that God has made, and we are driven to echo the judgment of God that it is all very good.

There is a tendency to forget where we have come from, so enamored are we of the sunlight. We must remember the darkness out of which we have emerged. We must remember it because it too is important in the process of growth and maturity. During the long wintering process, which all too often has been a time of discontent, our roots, like the roots of the trees around us, have been stretching and reaching further into the Ground of Being, sometimes but hopefully not always, without our being aware of what was happening to us.

All of which is a fairly accurate description and experience of the whole Paschal Mystery, the mystery of the dying and rising of Christ, and the mystery of our own dying and rising with him. We do not like the dying. Nor should we if we are healthy people. But the dying is an integral part of the whole picture and the whole mystery of our union with divinity. There is a darkness within all of us that we would rather not face and acknowledge. But it is an important part of us, and only by embracing it can we come to the full experience of the mystery. To the extent, says Gibran, that we have allowed pain to be carved into the depth of our being will we experience the depth of joy.

Happy spring, happy resurrection. It will be that to the extent that we have allowed the darkness and the dying to touch us.

~ *There is a darkness within all of us that we would rather not face and acknowledge. But it is an important part of us, and only by embracing it can we come to the full experience of the mystery.*

~ 15 ~

The Power of Powerlessness

Sooner or later every conflict can be seen for what it really is — a struggle for power. Oftentimes the conflict is camouflaged in other colors and is not immediately recognized as a power-struggle. Denial plays a large part in the masquerade, but the truth will finally emerge if there is some honesty on the part of those engaged in the conflict.

Vince Lombardi, the coach of the Green Bay Packers during their awesome winning years, used to say: "Winning isn't everything; it's the only thing." That philosophy may gain applause in the sporting arena, but it can be disastrous if it spills over into other areas of life. If, for example, that kind of thinking invades the spiritual walk, it deals the death blow to any kind of openness to the Spirit. If I must always win in life's battles, I am simply exercising the muscles of my own ego, without any kind of sensitivity to others or to my own responsibility to seek what God asks of me. I close my real self off to what is right for building the Kingdom, and simply become preoccupied with building my own glass kingdom. I must defend and protect my own kingdom, lest anyone see through my macho mask and see me for what I really am — a self-centered, egotistical, neurotic caricature of my real self. What I am doing is confusing control and freedom. That sort of thing is excusable in children who are flexing their inner muscles in an attempt to find themselves and to establish their own identity. But more is expected of adults who should be acting in a more mature way, with a consequent wisdom born of God.

The truth is that freedom comes only with losing ourselves in Him whose power upholds the universe. Jesus made it very clear, over and over again, in the Gospel: lose yourself in Me and you will find yourself. If I am always concerned about winning in life; if I am constantly trying to prove my worth, I have not yet understood the ingredients of spiritual growth. In forgetting myself and focusing on the goodness of God in gifting me with all that I am and all that I have — which is the only true view of myself — I begin to experience what true freedom is. I begin to free myself from the constraints and compulsions of having to be perfect — or, more correctly, of trying to make others believe that I am perfect.

The only kind of power that Jesus speaks of in the Gospel is the power to be powerless and the power to serve. The power to dominate others has *nothing* to do with what it means to be a disciple of Jesus; it is a kind of power that is foreign to the meaning of the Gospel.

The ultimate symbol of powerlessness is, of course, the cross. And Jesus tells us that the only way to release the power of the Spirit within us is to choose to embrace the cross ourselves and to follow the path of powerlessness. That's the foolishness of God. And therein lies wisdom. As Paul says, the foolishness of God is wiser than the wisdom of men.

> ~ *The power to dominate others has* nothing *to do with what it means to be a disciple of Jesus; it is a kind of power that is foreign to the meaning of the Gospel.*

~ 16 ~

Words from the Cross

O FATHER, what have I done to deserve this? I tried to do your will. I always took the time to be with you before making any important decisions. I thought I was doing the right thing. Was it really the right thing? Was I really only doing my thing?

Where are you, Father, now that I need you? You said you would be with me always. But, Father, I cannot feel you. I cannot find you. This desolation is overwhelming. The pain! I cannot breathe. I heave with the pain all over my body.

Where are all my friends? Have they all left me in this hour of need? I counted on them to be loyal, to carry on my work of bringing life to a lifeless world. Has all of my work been in vain, Father? I wanted them to know you as I know you. I wanted them to know the intimacy of your love. I wanted them to know the depth of your longing to be the center of their life. O Father, has it all been in vain? Has the dream that I fed them for so long gone up in smoke? Was it all an illusion? A puff of smoke? Was there any real fire?

The pain. O Father, the pain. Why have you left me? Why have all my friends left me except these few? Mother, how I love you! Always faithful. Always there. John, precious John! Where have they all gone? I tried to teach them the truth that you gave me. I thought they understood. I thought they would be faithful. Did I ask too much? Did they really understand? Father, forgive them. If they really understood, they would never have run away. Forgive Judas. Forgive Peter. Let them remember me with love.

Love! I tried to teach them to love. Just a few hours ago we were all together around the table. The bread, the wine. My body and blood. Was it too much for them to understand? Will they make the connection between the supper and my death? O Father, I am dying. Will they remember that they must lay down their lives for one another? Will they remember that I would be with them, live in them, wherever they went, whatever they did? Father, forgive them. Forgive them.

Forgive *me*. Did I really do all you gave me to do? Did I always do it for you, for the Kingdom? I am so thirsty. I cannot breathe. Give me strength, Father. I want to die right. I want them all to remember me. I want them all to be with us in our Kingdom.

Take care of my mother. Take care of John and Magdalen. Take care of them all. Let them remember me with love. Let them continue to believe in the Kingdom even as they watch me die.

O Father, take me home. Into your hands I give myself. Into your hands. Now. Always. The pain. I am yours. O Father!

~ *Will they remember that they must lay down their lives for one another? Will they remember that I would be with them, live in them, wherever they went, whatever they did?*

~ 17 ~

Eastering

Some people — perhaps most people — die long before their obituary appears in the newspaper. Jesus, too, died long before he was nailed to a tree.

These statements stand at the opposite ends of the spectrum of life. In the first instance, I speak of the fact that the desire to live, the zest for life, has died within people with the result that they simply drift passively through the hours of life. They are simply surviving, spectators waiting for kind death to claim them. This state in old, disabled, disoriented people is sad enough. But when this malaise and apathy strike people who are well and have great potential for participating in the excitement of life, it is pathetic.

In the case of Jesus, he died long before his death on the cross. He died because his heart was broken: he saw too much of human potential that went unused or was used to diminish life. He saw with the heart, with the inner eyes of love, and it killed him.

When Jesus' life on earth was completed; when his mission to open the eyes of the blind was finished, he unleashed the power of his Spirit on the world so that his work might be continued in and through us, his friends. His dying and rising became the mystery into which we, his friends, were plunged. In dying to our selfishness, we rise with Jesus to a new level of living and loving in the Father's Kingdom.

Eastering means that we see the meaning of life through the eyes of Jesus; that we see the world lit up with the presence of a loving Father; that we know we are unconditionally loved by God and we *must* respond lovingly to his constant call to a deeper life with him; and that we *must* share that joy of intimacy with God with our brothers and sisters.

To be eastered by Jesus, then, translates into an enthusiasm for life in all its forms. Beneath the surface of life, there is steadfast hope and joy which is founded on the surety of a living God who has invested himself intimately in the affairs of his creatures. That hope and joy can never be taken from us in spite of the tragedies of sin that surround us, and in spite of the changing moods that are part of what it means to be human.

The dreams we have for God are only a shadow of the dreams he has for us, only a shadow of what can be if we but follow his eastering Spirit.

"If we have died with Christ, we believe that we are also to live with him...His death was death to sin, once for all; his life is life for God. In the same way, you must consider yourselves dead to sin but alive for God in Christ Jesus" (Rom 6:8, 10, 11).

~ *Eastering means that we see the meaning of life through the eyes of Jesus; that we see the world lit up with the presence of a loving Father; that we know we are unconditionally loved by God and we* must *respond lovingly to his constant call to a deeper life with him; and that we* must *share that joy of intimacy with God with our brothers and sisters.*

~ 18 ~

Down the Up Staircase

Most of us, most of the time, are like the disciples of Jesus: we are preoccupied with ourselves and our own little worlds while he is trying to teach us divine wisdom. While he attempts to teach us how to go *down* the ladder, we are thinking of how we might climb *up* the ladder.

Time after time when the situation presents itself in the Gospel, Jesus has to call the disciples together and remind them of what the Kingdom is about. He takes a child in his arms and says: "Unless your heart is converted and you become like this little child, you will not enter the Kingdom." In fact, without Jesus-eyes we don't even know that the Kingdom is there. Without Jesus-eyes we are unable to pierce beyond the reality that faces us and see the world lit up with the presence of the Father. *With* Jesus-eyes, the invisible world begins to be, as it should, much more real than the visible world.

Jesus did not cling to his equality with God but *emptied* himself, Paul says, becoming like us in all things except sin. "And being as all people are, he was humbler yet, even to accepting death...on a cross" (Phil 2).

Jesus came *down* the ladder to show us how to rise to a right relationship with God and with each other. He came, he said, to serve, not to be served; to be our friend, not to lord it over us. To choose to be a disciple of Jesus and a friend of his is to come *down* the ladder and to be unaffected by the constant allure of a world that is at enmity with God. It is to keep one's feet firmly upon the earth as the locus of the Kingdom and to recognize our origin in the earth.

In humbling ourselves and emptying ourselves of our selfishness, the scales begin to fall from our eyes and we begin to understand who we really are. And we begin to see that all we are and have is the gift of a gracious God, and that we could do nothing to make ourselves worthy of such a gift. That is humility (from the Latin word *humus*, meaning earth), seeing the truth about God and ourselves and living that truth in daily life.

Humility, then, is the basis of our life with God and with one another. Everything good springs from that. From it, all the joy of being alive flows; and we respond to life, not from a greedy and possessive heart, but with a grateful heart.

> ~ *To choose to be a disciple of Jesus and a friend of his is to come* down *the ladder and to be unaffected by the constant allure of a world that is at enmity with God. It is to keep one's feet firmly upon the earth as the locus of the Kingdom and to recognize our origin in the earth.*

~ 19 ~

Compassion Brings Life

MEISTER ECKHART says that we may call God love, we may call Him goodness; but the best name for God is compassion. And Jesus, in his parable of the prodigal son, gives us a true picture of our Father-God: a loving father who throws his arms around his son even before the son has a chance to ask for forgiveness.

Compassion is having a drive, a passion to extend understanding and forgiveness to those who are in need of it. More: it even goes so far as to find an excuse for those who go astray. That's what Jesus did from the cross: "Father, forgive them for they don't know what they are doing." To break out of the prison of self and to stand under another (which is the best position to understand another), is the work of a godly person. To seek, further, an excuse for others' behavior is to enter into complete union with God.

The stumbling block for most people in extending compassion to others is their inability to accept compassion for themselves. If I haven't allowed myself to experience compassion, there is little likelihood that I will be able to extend compassion to others. A compassionate person, therefore, is one who has first known the depth of God's mercy and compassion.

Compassion is putting aside one's tendency toward preoccupation with self and entering the world of another. It is to become vulnerable with those who are vulnerable; to become powerless with those who are powerless; to become sad with those who are sad. It is to go where there is pain and hurt and to be willing to stay there to share the brokenness. This does not mean that we enjoy suffering; that would not be normal or natural. It simply means that we are willing to embrace the pain because we know that sharing it brings new life and new love.

When we show compassion to another, we are able to experience the truth of what Paul says: "I live, now not I, but Christ lives in me." In surrendering our greedy ego to the One who is Love, we find our true self, our noble self in Him. We walk tall in the joy and freedom that compassion births in us. We lay aside selfish competition with others and rejoice in their surprising goodness.

~ *Compassion is having a drive, a passion to extend understanding and forgiveness to those who are in need of it. More: it even goes so far as to find an excuse for those who go astray.*

~ 20 ~

Sounds of Silence

RECENTLY I HEARD a new (for me) term on the radio: *information overload*. Catchy, that. It was used in the commercial for *Time* magazine. "Make time for *Time*," it said. The message is, of course, that if we read *Time*, we will not have to read anything else, thereby avoiding that terrible plague, information-overload.

If catch-words do not aim at the truth, or if they contain only half-truths, are they worth bothering about? I don't suppose that it ever occurred to the editors of *Time* that people might think that there is something beyond their magazine's information worthy of their or our attention.

Like silence, for instance. When was the last time you felt surfeited with all the noise around you and within you and just wanted to sit? What did you do about it?

There's the rub. Probably the last time you felt that way, you walked over to turn on the radio or TV, or went to get a book, or hurried to cash in on the latest sale at Sears — or maybe even picked up *Time*. Anything to avoid the boredom of having nothing to do, no information to absorb.

Why not just sit! Notice I said *sit!* Not sit and think, or sit and stew, or sit and laugh, or sit and do anything. Try it. You might find it challenging.

What I'm getting at is that so many of us in this anxiety-ridden, compulsively work-oriented culture of ours find it difficult to enjoy silence and would rather do anything than be quiet. It's a rather non-flattering sign of our times. And it points to our insecurity and rootlessness.

Unless we are rooted in God, and rooted in the only sure way of listening to God — namely, silence — then we are doomed to spend our lives standing at the window of life and watching the world go by. The only participative entry into the life that God offers us and wants us to enjoy is through silence and "in touchness" with Him who fills the world with the sounds of silence and ultimate meaning.

Information doesn't usually feed our spirit. But communion always does. And the only way to communion — with ourselves, with others, with God — is through silence.

It strikes me that most of the first part of our lives is spent filling our heads with information. The last part — and the most important part — is spent emptying our heads of all that trivia so that our hearts may be free to learn wisdom — in silence.

~ *The only participative entry into the life that God offers us and wants us to enjoy is through silence and "in touchness" with Him who fills the world with the sounds of silence and ultimate meaning.*

~ 21 ~

Prisoners of the Lord

LATELY I'VE BEEN SEEING more deeply how unfree all of us really are.

Jesus came to free us up from all the compulsions that we are heir to in the human condition — and we remain shackled. Obviously there is something wrong. Jesus has not failed in *his* mission; *we* have failed in responding to the gift of freedom that he has won for us.

So long as we continue to attempt to impress others, to outdo them, to compare ourselves to others, we are falling victim to our own unfreedoms and our own shackles. To that extent we are failing to act out of our own center, which is the God in whom we live and move and have our being. We render Him and ourselves helpless. We *react* to external stimuli instead of acting out of our own graced center. To the degree that we do that, we become less human, which means that we become less divine than what our God has called us, and wants us, to be. We become prisoners of ourselves.

Ironically, the only key that can free us from the prison into which we ourselves have walked is the key of being prisoners of the Lord. As we surrender all that we are and have to him (*all* of which is his gift to us in the first place), he frees us up to become more ourselves, and consequently more like him who is freedom itself.

It should make us sad and fill us with a healthy kind of shame that we have lived so long and understood so little of life. But it is comforting to know that, sooner or later, most people do wake up. It is comforting to realize that our God is so patient with us. Even if our awakening is later rather than sooner, the important thing is that our moment of enlightenment has at last arrived. That it comes at *all* is much more important than *when* it comes. God, I'm sure, is much more interested in what we learn from our mistakes and what we do as a result of the mistakes than in the mistakes themselves.

As the old axiom goes, we grow too soon old and too late smart. And that's all right. Just so, somewhere along the line, we get smart. That's divine.

> ~ *Ironically, the only key that can free us from the prison into which we ourselves have walked is the key of being prisoners of the Lord. As we surrender all that we are and have to him (all of which is his gift to us in the first place), he frees us up to become more ourselves, and consequently more like him who is freedom itself.*

~ 22 ~

Take Off Your Shoes

"To act in the world as if it were a sanctuary is to make it reverential and sacred, and is to make yourself elevated and meaningful. What the universe becomes depends on you. Treat it like a machine and it becomes a machine. Treat it like a divine place and it becomes a divine place. Treat it indifferently and ruthlessly and it becomes an indifferent and ruthless place. Treat it with love and care and it becomes a loving and caring place." So said Henryk Skolimowski. No truer words have ever been spoken to a world that is ripping apart at the seams. The violence that has burst upon us so universally is only an indication that we carry within ourselves the incendiaries of frightening eruptions more furious and destructive than Mt. Pinitubo. In an age when we are more alert and sensitive to injustices on every level, we strike out at them in words and actions that know no limits. The time has greatly diminished — and thank God for that — when oppressive governments and organizations that thrived on enforcing unjust laws through force of fear will no longer be tolerated for the most part. Let us hope that irreverent extremes have been reached, and that we can now start to swing back to a saner center.

It's good to go back to Elizabeth Barrett Browning's marvelous little poem that illuminates life as it really is, and probably as it always will be:

> *Earth's crammed with heaven*
> *And every common bush afire with God.*

> *Those who see take off their shoes;*
> *The rest sit round it and pluck blackberries.*

Perhaps that is the answer: we do not see very well. We do not see that the world, as coming from the hands of a loving Creator, is worthy of our care and reverence. We somehow have come to believe that we own the world and can trash it as we wish. Our eyes are at last being opened, and we see that we cannot do that without the earth striking back at us. On the positive side, as St. Francis taught us way back in the 13th century, all of earth's creatures are our brothers and sisters, deserving our care and reverence. I recall a photographer who used to spend hours with flowers, trying to make them feel comfortable before taking their pictures.

The truth is that we own nothing except our sins. All has been given us on loan; everything is the gift of a loving and gracious God. He asks us to take care of this wonderful playground, to be responsible stewards of creation, to see that life is nourished and preserved.

Only a profound understanding of these truths and an individual commitment to caring for the earth and for one another can bring us the inner joy that we seek. That joy is the fruit of a grateful heart which recognizes that all is gift.

Solzhenitsyn said it well: "The only salvation of humanity lies in everyone being concerned with everything everywhere."

~ *Earth's crammed with heaven*
  And every common bush afire with God.
  Those who see take off their shoes;
  The rest sit round it and pluck blackberries.
  　　　　　　—E. B. Browning

~ 23 ~

Leaving the Garbage Behind

I LIKE TO VISIT the playground of the grade school next to our house of prayer. The little pre-schoolers have a great time laughing and shouting with joy on the swings and slide. One day a little boy asked me, as I stooped to pick up some scraps of paper on the ground (as is my wont because of my strong environmental awareness), "Are you the garbage man?"

Hesitating for a moment because the question caught me off-guard, I replied with some amount of surety, "Yes, I am."

Afterwards, as I reflected on the question and answer, I thought how right it all was. That's what I really am — a garbage man.

So much of my time as a priest is spent listening to the load of garbage that people are carrying around. Some have been carrying their garbage for months, even years, and it has affected their bodies as well as their hearts. Some people's eyes are muddy because of that; some have the frightened eyes of a rabbit being chased; some, knowing that the truth is not in them, have wandering eyes when they talk to you. But then there are some whose eyes are clear and confident and compassionate because they have learned to be gentle with their garbage and let it speak to them about life.

Such are the wise ones. They are the ones who have not allowed their garbage to overwhelm them. They have accepted the fact that life is hard as well as beautiful, and that they must accept the bitter and the sweet. They are the ones whom life has matured. They have learned how to give because they have leaned how to receive.

One word spoken from a pure and gentle heart is worth more than a million words spoken from a chaotic and selfish heart. You know that right away if you are in touch with the Spirit who dwells in you. Your spirit is touched and you have been blessed when you hear a word from a person like Jesus and those who are faithful to his teaching. The word becomes like oil oozing over your whole being, anointing you, healing you, making you more whole than you were before.

The good news is that even when we listen to others' garbage, we don't have to hold on to it. Jesus said we could and should give it over to him. He apparently has a way of absorbing it all without allowing it to burden him. He's amazing.

Those who are wise will learn from the garbage they experience and let it soften and cleanse their hearts so they can speak from the abundant life that Jesus has won for them. The rest will only get more stooped.

> *~ The good news is that even when we listen to others' garbage, we don't have to hold on to it. Jesus said we could and should give it over to him. He apparently has a way of absorbing it all without allowing it to burden him. He's amazing.*

~ 24 ~

Roofing

ROOFS NEVER REALLY interested me. Never, that is, until I landed at Sancta Clara Monastery (Poor Clares) in Canton, Ohio. There, on top the lovely old Tudor mansion, was a slate roof, the likes of which I had never seen before. Each piece, I found out, is screwed in its place — some pieces big, some small; some thick, some thin. And all of them are irregular in size.

One of my retreatants recently called my attention to this and made a marvelous meditation one day on how the roof of Sancta Clara was a mirror of the Church. Indeed, of humanity. The roof, despite the irregularity of each piece (or because of it), formed a beautiful whole, like an intricate tapestry.

That, I think, is what I love about the Sisters at Sancta Clara: the roof over them is a forceful reminder of the uniqueness of each Sister. As I have come to know and love them individually (and to thank God constantly for sending me to minister and be brother to them), I am struck by how all of them fit together to form a microcosm of the Church. The Sisters are a never-ending source of delight to me because as soon as I think I have learned all there is to know about them, they surprise me by showing me an aspect of themselves that I haven't seen before.

Paradoxically, this is precisely the kind of unity that Jesus prayed for, as recorded in John 17, shortly before he went to his death and glorification. Jesus prayed that we would be one in him as he was one in and with the Father. And that unity would be effected, not by all of us looking alike or talking alike or seeing alike, but by each one of us allowing ourselves to be molded and formed into the unique persons God wants us to be. Only in that way, bonded together deeply in Jesus, could we reflect the facets of perfect love that divinity reached down to our toes to touch.

I never cease to marvel at the words of Charles de Foucauld, who said in effect that we dare not limit our view of others by what we see and know of them; that we must believe everything of everyone and hope in them always; and that we must be love in a world that does not know how to love.

"A thing of beauty is a joy forever," Keats said. I wonder if he would include roofs in that. I certainly would.

~ *"To love anyone is to hope in him for always. From the moment at which we begin to judge anyone, to limit our confidence in him; from the moment at which we identify him with what we know of him and so reduce him to that, we cease to love him and he ceases to be able to become better. We should expect everything of everyone. We must dare to be love in a world that does not know how to love."*

—Charles de Foucauld

~ 25 ~

The Roar of Pentecost

PENTECOST THIS YEAR was the most memorable of my life. I spent it with my dearest soul-friend, Sister Joan Marie, who was in Cincinnati, nearing the end of a three-month internship program in Franciscan spiritual direction. It was a five-hour drive, and well worth it.

The morning liturgy at St. Anthony's Shrine in Cincinnati was magnificent. The Franciscan Friars there were obviously in touch with the Spirit, and each man and woman present seemed to know his/her role in the service perfectly. Joy resounded and rebounded off the walls of that church.

Joanie and I spent the rest of the day spontaneously as the Spirit directed us. We prayed, we shared what God seemed to be saying to us; we enjoyed in silence the brilliance of the day in an ancient cemetery filled with ornate, huge monuments and lovely, meandering lagoons. At one point in the afternoon, as we sat on the grass by one of the small lagoons, a mother duck waddled over to us just as we were nearing the end of Vespers. Strangely, she was all alone, apart from the other ducks, and made herself right at home with us. With her beak, she kept rooting around in the grass for bugs to eat. Then she beaked up and down my socks and shoes as we watched in amazement at her fearlessness. When we prayed Francis' Canticle of Brother Sun and again when we opened with the words of the Our Father, our little friend's head perked up from the grass and she became very still, as if she recognized a solemn moment. It was. When Joanie and I took a few steps toward our car, pausing to talk again about the overwhelming beauty of the day, there at Joanie's foot was the duck again, sitting and seeming to say, "It's been good to be with you."

The rest of Pentecost was one comedy of errors after another. Since neither of us knew Cincinnati very well, we kept getting lost. We laughed so hard with each other until, at the end of the day, we were "exhausted-refreshed" and our bellies hurt.

The day was a powerful reminder that the Spirit can work on us when we take life seriously — either in a heart-to-heart sharing or in laughing heartily at the incongruities of life. And oftentimes, more becomes clear about the meaning of life in laughing together than at any other time. The Spirit has his ways.

~ *The Spirit can work on us when we take life seriously — either in a heart-to-heart sharing or in laughing heartily at the incongruities of life. And oftentimes, more becomes clear about the meaning of life in laughing together than at any other time. The Spirit has his ways.*

~ 26 ~

Releasing the Spirit

THERE'S A REPRODUCTION of a lovely painting in the foyer of our Friary here in Canton. It's called "Boy and Crow" by the Finnish artist Aksele Gallen-Kallala. It shows a little boy, perhaps six years old, gazing in wonder at the bird at his feet. The boy is raggedly dressed, standing in a rather stark area of Finland. The suggestion is that, while the boy is very poor to all outward appearances, he is enormously rich inside; he has discovered the beauty of God's creation.

Parenthetically, the painting belonged to my mother and was her favorite. Perhaps she loved it so much because it reminded her of me, her only son, or of what she hoped I would be.

At any rate, it is now my favorite painting, for obvious and not-so-obvious reasons. What I see in the painting is an excellent example of what I would describe as contemplative prayer. The boy is drawn out of himself by the sight of the bird, held in awe by its otherness. He is taking a long, loving look at the real. That's contemplation. It's as simple — and demanding — as that.

We have all had at times some rather fuzzy notions about contemplative prayer. We have seen it as something esoteric and unusual, reserved for only a few, notably those in monasteries. But it is also for those in the marketplace. For we are *all* called to intimacy with our God. We are *all* called to be contemplatives. We are *all* called to live life reflectively and deeply.

Contemplative prayer is as simple as sitting in silence at

the feet of the Lord and listening to his voice, gazing at his face through the lynx-like eyes of faith. It is to get in contact with the living God who has taken up his residence within us — to be hushed in the presence of the overwhelming mystery that God is. And that life is.

While this kind of prayer is supremely simple, it is also very demanding. The price is high: an enormous amount of discipline. It requires a willingness on our part to take the time that is necessary to let God speak to our hearts. Without silence and solitude — a good dose of it everyday — there is no way that we can be attentive to the God who wants to reveal more and more of himself in order that we may be happy and fulfilled.

St. Teresa of Avila used a very simple exercise to get her into prayer. Imagine, she says, you see Jesus coming to you and looking at you lovingly and humbly. Let him love you. Let him get down on his knees and wash your feet. How does that make you feel? How do you react and respond to that? Rest in his love for you — a love that is total gift, something that could never be earned and is absolutely unconditional, regardless of your unworthiness.

You have experienced the humility of God. You have experienced contemplative prayer.

~ *Contemplative prayer is as simple as sitting in silence at the feet of the Lord and listening to his voice, gazing at his face through the lynx-like eyes of faith. It is to get in contact with the living God who has taken up his residence within us — to be hushed in the presence of the overwhelming mystery that God is. And that life is.*

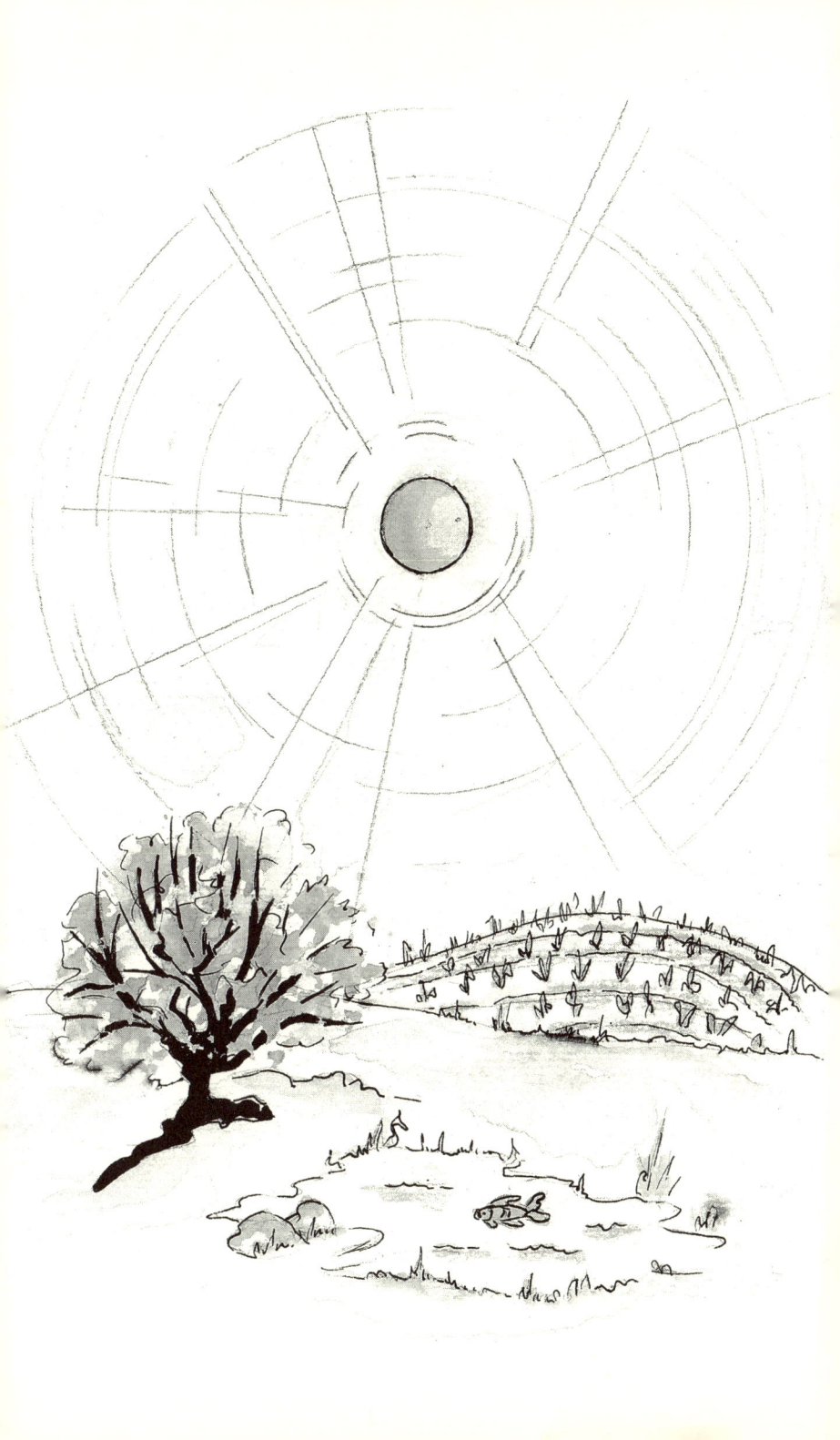

~ 27 ~

Fountain of Life

ST. BONAVENTURE, in typical Franciscan fashion, is effusive in his love for the sacred heart of Jesus:

"O indescribable beauty of the most high God and purest radiance of eternal light! Life that gives all life, light that is the source of every other light, preserving in everlasting splendor the myriad flames that have shone before the throne of your divinity from the dawn of time! Eternal and inaccessible fountain, clear and sweet stream flowing from a hidden spring, unseen by mortal eye! None can fathom your depths nor survey your boundaries, none can measure your breadth, nothing can sully your purity. From you flows the river which gladdens the city of God and makes us cry out with joy and thanksgiving in hymns of praise to you, for we know by our own experience that with you is the source of life, and in your light we see light."

From the depths of that sacred heart of Jesus come these words:

No matter how much you try to capture the depth of my love for you in words, you will always fail. There is simply no way that words are capable of expressing what my heart feels for you. Not even the lofty words of Bonaventure.

You must believe that, my friends. That is the most profound act of faith you could ever make. I am not speaking of those truths that you utter, for the most part unthinkingly, in your liturgies. That is important, to be sure. But infinitely beyond that clear and distinct doctrine is your unshakable belief that I love you, not in spite of your sinfulness, but because of it.

Many people are able to express the doctrines of faith clearly, but they have stopped there and so their knowledge has not really affected their actions. The longest journey is the journey from the head to the heart. Set out on that journey, my friends. And never stop listening to the truths that can be heard only by those who take the time to be silent. Choose to be alone with me during the best part of your day, so that I may reveal the secrets of divinity to you. That alone will bring rest and peace to your weary hearts. That alone will make you want to take off your shoes and tread the earth with reverence and treat one another with the dignity that is yours as children of God. Never forget that you are a temple of the Spirit, that my Father and I have come to dwell within you and will never leave you, and that my kingdom is within you and all around you. Open your eyes to that kingdom, and love it into lived reality.

Let me lead you into ever-greener pastures of life. Let me be your shepherd. Give joy to my heart by being all that you can be with my grace. That will make you happy. And you will find that the more you share my gifts with others, the more you open yourself to an increase of joy and fulfillment.

Remember, my friends, I love you, not because you are good but because I am good. I have laid down my life for you. I have loved you to death. Now love one another with that same love, and your hearts will find rest. That is the key: rest, rest in my loving heart.

~ *The longest journey is the journey from the head to the heart. Set out on that journey, my friends. And never stop listening to the truths that can be heard only by those who take the time to be silent.*

~ 28 ~

Getting It Together

THERE IS A STORY of a woman who sat reflectively on a large rock by the ocean for several hours. Afterwards she recorded these words of her experience:

>cominginness
>goingoutness
>everthereness

Remarkably, she captured the whole of what life is meant to be in three words. For life is all about coming home to our inner self, going out of our self to enter life as it unfolds around us, and attempting to stay present to that life as it happens without losing the inner vision.

As I listen to the Gospel, that is the picture I get of Jesus, who was able to pull that off perfectly. He was constantly in touch with the Father, knew what he was about because he knew who he was and why he was sent; and, as a consequence, he was able through that inner strength to meet the needs of every person he met and every situation he encountered. He was perfectly balanced at all times. That is the challenge that Jesus confronts us with if we are to be his disciples.

Even if we are extraordinarily gifted by nature and grace, we can never come to that perfect balance that Jesus experienced. The important thing to remind ourselves of is that *Jesus doesn't expect us to*. The challenge, nonetheless, remains, and will remain to the end of time.

Perhaps all the mistakes of human history can be reduced

to this: either too much extraversion or too much introversion. Of the two, probably the most and worst mistakes have been due to too much extroversion, though that certainly is debatable.

To keep the inner and outer world in good (not perfect) balance, we must follow the path that Jesus the Way set for us. Often he spent the nights in communion with the Father, away from everyone and in places that were inaccessible to other people. I suspect that if the truth were told, *that* took up much of his time on earth, perhaps even most of it. The Gospels necessarily only hint at the answer to this question.

Because Jesus' inner life was so consumingly rich with the vision of Truth, he was able to meet all the demands of life as he found it in his segment of human history. We are not so fortunate. We struggle constantly to maintain that balance, and in one way or another we fail. And that is expected.

But what God expects of us is that we constantly accept the challenge and renew the struggle. That calls for a good dose of silence and prayer in our daily life. We are expected to be faithful to that every day. If that is not possible to us, then we are too busy; and we need to rearrange our priorities in order to come into a state of homeostasis.

The acceleration with which we live and the technology that feeds it have contrived to reduce us into being robots incapable of a rich interior life. The violence that is the result of this inability to integrate life as it unfolds means a world falling apart, disjointed, and chaotic. The stress is too much; it is breaking us down instead of building us up. A healthy stress and tension between us human beings and our environment, as intended by God in the beginning and forevermore, is the result of the good balance of "cominginness" and "goingoutness." Only in that way can we come into the "everthereness" that Jesus challenges us with.

~ *cominginness*
goingoutness
everthereness

~ 29 ~

Where Is Your Heart?

"LET US GO THEN, you and I / When the evening is stretched out against the sky / Like a patient etherized upon a table." Thus we are ushered into the sick world of T. S. Eliot's "The Love Song of J. Alfred Prufrock."

A sick world indeed — a world of make-believe, a world of chatter without end, a world of defending oneself against the encroaching sickle of time. Prufrock becomes a symbol of the inanity of modern humanity searching for meaning in the familiar places of trinkets and toys and everything shiny. Anything is used to avoid the overwhelming question of what life is really about and how we deal with and transcend reality.

It is this kind of experience of inner sickness and emptiness that God often uses to bring us to our knees in search of the light. Those who come to God in that way — in a spirit of humility (which is the truth about him/her and ourselves) — will go away enlightened and whetted for further light. They have found at last that God is the only one who can satisfy their inner longing for meaning and fulfillment in the midst of the apparent meaninglessness of life. Those who snuff out the light — both theirs and others' — will go away unenlightened and searching endlessly and vainly for some other way of ending the pain of guilt and fear. Just around the corner, they say to themselves, happiness is waiting for them. And so the search goes on. And the emptiness and unhappiness.

If God permitted you to make one request, what would you ask for? Your response to that question will reveal just where you are with God and with yourself. It will show you where your heart is. "Where your treasure is," Jesus said, "there your heart is also" (Mt 6:21). It's foolproof.

What turned Solomon on when God asked him that question was not some trinket of power or prestige or wealth or ambitious maneuver. Nothing of the kind; nothing that you and I, in our selfishness, would probably ask for. Solomon asked only for an understanding heart to deal with the people that God had entrusted to his kingly (servant) care (1 Kgs 3:9). That says a great deal about the magnanimous heart that Solomon had and his priorities in life. There lies wisdom.

So what turns you on? Be honest, and be careful what you ask for. God may see fit to give it to you.

~ *If God permitted you to make one request, what would you ask for? Your response to that question will reveal just where you are with God and with yourself. It will show you where your heart is.*

~ 30 ~

Prayer Napping

I JUST GOT UP from a nap. As usual, I feel calm and reflective and energized, ready to live again.

That daily nap is really important. It's a pause in the action that refreshes my body, my mind, my heart. Without it, I would only drag myself through the remainder of the day, doing what I have to do without being much together and without much awareness of what I was doing and why I was doing it. With it, I can keep the Lord in focus and can continue to pray to him through all the rest of the things that I do that day.

My daily nap is a powerful announcement to the world around me that I am listening to my body, which has told me to let go of everything and fall into the arms of the living God. And the Lord does indeed give to his beloved in sleep, as we hear in Ps 127. He has proved that to me over and over again when I am stymied over something; I simply sleep on it for a while, and I find the answer as soon as I awaken. He never fails.

The prayer of napping, as Edward Hays calls it, is something that Jesus must have allowed himself quite often because he is always so alert to the needs of life around him. The best example of course is the incident described in Mark 4:35–41, where Jesus fell asleep in the boat. A storm came up and the disciples became very fearful of the ominous sky and the swelling waves. The disciples awakened Jesus, and he remonstrated with them about having such little faith. Jesus evidently felt that he didn't have to be saving the world every minute of every day, that he could safely relax and entrust his life to his heavenly Father without having to prove his worth at all times and in all places, that the exorbitant and sometimes unreasonable expectations of others were not worth worrying about.

Letting go is so difficult for some of us because we have such a poor perception of our own worth. We need to keep up appearances. We need to impress others with our untiring devotedness to work. We end up being neurotically compulsive workers because we are so insecure about ourselves. The world will fall apart, we think, if we do not finish this job right now. Someone will find out the staggering truth that we are not perfect. That would be the end of the road for us.

Thomas Merton said on one occasion that we are not truly poor until we consider ourselves expendable. It's really marvelous how a simple thing like the prayer of napping can bring us into a profound and freeing experience of the truth of being expendable. The world would then be a better place to live in and love in. And our poverty would be turned into a richness that would defy explaining.

~ *Letting go is so difficult for some of us because we have such a poor perception of our own worth.*

~ *Thomas Merton said on one occasion that we are not truly poor until we consider ourselves expendable.*

~ 31 ~

Addicted to Jesus

WE ARE ALL NEUROTICS. All of us are addicts of one kind or another. The things I am addicted to are bran muffins, Russell Stover sour lemon wedges (one a day, at bedtime), and dead leaves. (I don't eat the leaves, but I cannot not pick them up in the fall of the year. Dead things, like people, are meant to be buried, I keep hearing. Our God is a God of the living, not of the dead.)

I have not yet found a lemon-drop treatment center to relieve me partially of my addictions. But I keep looking. Someone, somewhere, somehow will take pity on us lemon-drop junkies and erect a center to treat us hapless people.

I have another addiction that I haven't mentioned. I'm addicted to Jesus. Every time I think of Jesus or mention his name or hear it mentioned, my mouth starts watering and my lips start smacking. Jesus turns me on.

Wouldn't it be a delightful world if everyone were addicted to Jesus? We'd have a world full of hope and love instead of illusions and hate; a world full of sensitive, loving people who would watch out for and care for one another instead of suspicious people carefully guarding their own turf, people whose gaze would be focused not on themselves and their own petty hurts, but on Him who can bind up our wounds and heal us with a simple gaze of his compassionate eyes.

I doubt that there will ever be a need for a Jesus treatment center. I would be willing, in fact, to stake my life on that. We can never get too much of Jesus. The paradox is that the more we lose ourselves in Jesus, the more clearly we discover who we are. And the more we discover who we are, the more whole and holier we become. That spells doom for any notion of a Jesus treatment center.

The trouble is, of course, that most of us most of the time don't know who we are. This produces the anxiety that drives us to alcohol, drugs, sex — anything that can make us forget our miserable selves for a while. We haven't yet assimilated the truth that discovering ourselves means accepting our *whole* selves — not just the pretty part, but the ugly part; not just the flower, but the roots. If we are truly rooted in Jesus who is the Truth — we won't have to be checking ourselves out in the mirror every half hour; we won't need to worry about how we are coming across to people. (There's enough of that on the political scene to make us all nauseous.) We will *know* who we are and what we are about.

St. Paul says it so clearly: Put on the Lord Jesus Christ; let that mind be in you that was in Christ Jesus. I live, Paul says, yet not I, but Christ lives in me. That is the clearest statement of identity with Jesus and what it brings about. We live *in* Jesus, Paul keeps repeating; we *room* with him. We become so absorbed in him, so preoccupied with him, that on any given occasion of life, we know what we are to say and what we are to do because we know what Jesus would say and do. We allow Jesus the time and space he needs to set us free to be ourselves.

I like being addicted to Jesus. It's so much fun. As Geoff Hoyle said, "The fool strips away our preconceptions, so we can see the world as it might be." Maybe we need more fools for Christ's sake.

~ *We can never get too much of Jesus. The paradox is that the more we lose ourselves in Jesus, the more clearly we discover who we are. And the more we discover who we are, the more whole and holier we become.*

~ 32 ~

We Are Pilgrims

ST. FRANCIS SAYS in his Rule of 1223: "The friars shall not appropriate anything to themselves, neither house nor place nor anything. Instead, as pilgrims and strangers in this world who serve the Lord in poverty and humility, they should go begging alms confidently" (Chap. 6).

This started me on a reflection of what it means to be a pilgrim. We use that word *pilgrim* a great deal, and it always fascinates me. It's a beautiful word. And its meaning is even more beautiful in the Franciscan context.

Francis is insisting that we must let go of everything that we so easily cling to because of our basic insecurity. That can involve a terrible wrenching, a terrible struggle that can go on — and usually does — for years. But that is the price of freedom. And that is precisely, I think, what Francis wants not only for his brothers but for all of us — the freedom to be all that we can be by nature and grace. Only then can we search out, without anything to distract us through ownership, the God who has first loved us and who continues to ravish our hearts. Only in the surrender of all that we are and have will we be free enough from every form of compulsivity to love freely and purely in return. That, as I see it, is essentially what a pilgrim is.

To be pilgrim, then, is to be, interiorly if not exteriorly, free from all that can distract us. It is to have a pure heart. It is to be a beggar. It is to be open to let the Lord do whatever he wants with us. It is to come with open hands and accept whatever is put in them. It is to seek *God* and not allow religious trappings and appendages of any sort, however "holy" they may seem to be, to get in the way.

To be pilgrim is to create a room inside for Jesus where he will be comfortable and very much at home. Francis did that. And that is why he owned the whole world.

~ *Only in the surrender of all that we are and have will we be free enough from every form of compulsivity to love freely and purely in return. That, as I see it, is essentially what a pilgrim is.*

~ *To be pilgrim is to create a room inside for Jesus where he will be comfortable and very much at home.*

~ 33 ~

Transformation

I'M LISTENING to the sounds around me. In the office just a few feet away, one of the secretaries is tapping on the electric typewriter. On the roof, some men are banging boards into submission. On the street, cars are zooming by. But here in the dining room, where I have chosen to write (don't ask why!), the tables and chairs and glasses and plates are silent, waiting for people to sit at or on or to use. The only thing that could distract me are the eerie, waving shadows that the leaves on the trees outside the dining room are making on the wall opposite me. I don't have to look at them. I don't even have to listen to the sounds around me. I can control that.

Once I have determined to move with the rhythm of the sounds instead of allowing them to annoy me and interrupt my train of thought, I have conquered them. They become the background music that I march to and flow with. Inside, I am still. Inside, I am at peace with the world. Thomas Merton said it well: "In joy, everything just as it is, whether 'for' or 'against': in peace, in universal acceptance, in Christ."

It bothers me when I see people walking or riding or jogging with earphones on. Not because they are listening to something, but because they are trying to do two things at once. That leads to a divided heart. It diminishes life within. We need to learn how to listen to, and enter into, the natural sounds around us, and allow them to transform us as they are transformed within us.

The most transforming sounds are the sounds of silence. "Be still and know that I am God" (Ps 46). It's the only way to come into a knowledge of God. In the beginning, we shut out the external sounds in order to get in touch with our hearts. That's the way of all flesh. There's no other way. If we stay with that regularly over a long period of time, we gradually discover that the real distractions in our quest for God are not so much the noises outside us, but the noises within us: our restless hearts that hanker for attention, our hungry egos that long for center-stage.

Meanwhile, the noise goes on. If our hearts have sought God long enough and hard enough, we come at last to see that we can, with poet Jessica Powers, "... by-pass all meadows that trap us with their poisonous flowers / and their soliciting pools / and winding lanes that skirt the only death." When that happens, what we now call noise becomes music to our tamed and transformed hearts.

~ *We need to learn how to listen to, and enter into, the natural sounds around us, and allow them to transform us as they are transformed within us.*

~ 34 ~

We Die without Poets

A LINE FROM *The Little Prince* continues to speak profoundly to me: "It is only with the heart that one sees rightly. What is essential is invisible to the eye." Seeing with the heart — looking deeper than what the eye is able to perceive — is the job of the poet. If there ever comes a time when we feel that we no longer need the poet in our culture — and I believe that we are precariously close to that time — then we have ceased to be a people of faith and hope and vision.

We need the poet to call us back continuously to where we have come from and where we are going. We die without insight, without meaning. We cannot grow on a continuous diet of consumerism, or by filling our senses with an infinite array of sensationalism. The world that is absorbed in the here-and-now and the tangible bombards us *ad nauseam* with the shiny boxes of tinsel that bring us instant gratification, and little else than that. The poet reminds us that this is not what fullness of life is all about. He reminds us that what we really desire is beyond the limits of our reach. He invites us to come home to ourselves and find rest in the God who has pitched his tent among us. We need him lest we perish.

A cynic is born of a culture that knows the price of everything and the value of nothing. He smells the flowers and looks for the coffin. A poet smells the flowers, marvels at their beauty, and longs to see who made them. He points the way to life.

Jesus was a poet. He not only pointed the way to life; he was the Way to Life. He knew what the lilies of the field proclaimed. He knew that the birds of the air were a rich symbol of our own desire to transcend what our eyes behold. He knew the value of a blade of grass. He paused to look at and listen to the reality around him and to allow it to touch him and speak to him of the Father's goodness.

Jesus taught us the poetry of life: that all who believed in him would never experience endless death, would know where they were going and why, would remain in the truth and know more of it as time unfolded, and would understand the relative value of things in a constantly changing world.

May Jesus give us clearer, cleaner hearts to see with. Hearts that respond to the beauty of all the Father has been pleased to gift us with.

~ *We need the poet to call us back continuously to where we have come from and where we are going.*

~ *He invites us to come home to ourselves and find rest in the God who has pitched his tent among us.*

~ 35 ~

The Ordinary Touch of Divinity

THE MORE SELF-INDULGENT we are during the extraordinary seasons of the year, the more the ordinary seasons escape us as significant. If we invest highly of ourselves in, for example, Christmas or Easter — and sate ourselves emotionally and materially in the process — the less we have to savor the ordinary seasons that follow these special feasts. The post-binge leaves us flat and restless. Often we yearn to continue the excited times; and as we attempt to do that, we rob ourselves of what the quiet and ordinary times can teach us of life. We drown out the Voice within that could bring peace, joy, and significance to the unspectacular life.

Actually, the terms "ordinary" and "extraordinary" are the human ways of looking at reality. There can be no such division in God's eyes; all events and situations in life are extraordinary because they are all shot through with divinity.

That's why we need God-eyes — eyes that can pierce the human and see the divine. Otherwise, we just sit around the common bushes and pluck blackberries instead of seeing the bushes afire with God. We are doomed, then, to walk through the human adventure with our eyes closed to the divinity that brings sparkle to life. If our eyes are open — touched with divinity — then the world is alive with the quiet sense of God's presence. We can then relax and enjoy the beauty of this marvelous playground that God has created for us.

Jesus has come to free us from the fear and self-concern

that constricts our vision and makes life more of a problem to be solved than a mystery to be embraced. As long as we continue to want to control life in all its aspects, the more our vision of what life can be is blurred and uneventful. As life becomes prosaic, *we* become prosaic; and we have nothing significant to offer others. There is only the boring, the humdrum, the everyday routine things that are repeated mindlessly day after day, year after year. We become, as a result, less free, more compulsive, more willful about all that we do. We become robots.

The power of a man like Thich Nhat Hanh, a Vietnamese Buddhist monk who lives with his followers in a community in southern France, is his disciplined ability to live fully in the present moment. I used to have a banner that read: "Never look back in anger, nor forward in fear, but around in awareness." That's the message that Hanh repeats. It sounds very simple, but it is in reality very hard to live. It requires an enormous measure of energy to dwell in the present moment, whatever it brings of God to us. It is an exercise in mindfulness.

Hanh's message is not new. Jesus constantly was getting at this when he said to his disciples over and over: "Do not be afraid." Fear is the opposite of faith and a barrier to love. "What is needed is trust," Jesus said. If I trust, my mind and heart are freed from worry and I can concentrate on just this moment of grace, responding lovingly to whatever the Lord is asking of me right now.

The past cannot be undone, the future is unpredictable. Only the present exists to accept with joy and trust. And if we are always looking for the spectacular, we will miss the grace of what is quietly ordinary.

> ~ *Actually, the terms "ordinary" and "extraordinary" are the human ways of looking at reality. There can be no such division in God's eyes; all events and situations in life are extraordinary because they are all shot through with divinity.*

~ 36 ~

Passion for Truth

THE CATHOLIC CHURCH is not as bad as some people say it is; nor is it as good as others say it is. Which is to say, the Church, like every other human institution, is not perfect. Which is also to say, the Holy Spirit is obviously able to break through some of the agendas of Church leaders when they are not looking or when (praise God!) they are praying and listening to the voice of the same Spirit.

I like to think that the Church of 1994 is not essentially different from the Church of 1215. Francis of Assisi was alive in 1215, when the decrees of the Lateran Council went into effect. He remembered the word that came to him from the cross at San Damiano: "Francis, rebuild my church, which, as you see, is falling into ruin."

Francis was well aware of the abuses in the church of 1215 — the same struggle for power, the same clericalism, sexism, patriarchalism, triumphalism. But fortified with the Lord's word to him, Francis decided that the only honorable course open to him, in his small effort to rebuild the Church, was to go *down* the ladder, not up it. He would aspire to be nobody, not somebody. He would choose the way that Jesus chose — the way of humility, the way of servanthood, the way of powerlessness. He would simply be a brother and a friend to all people and love them just as they were, with no attempt to change them in any way. He knew instinctively that people clamored for power out of a sense of their own insecurity. And they did all manner of prideful things to attract attention because they did not feel loved. Francis found all his security in the Lord who loved him even to the point of dying for him on a cross. That was all he needed. He would simply be love at the heart of the Church. He would stand counterculturally in the midst of a church that was crazed with power.

As a follower of Francis, I stand with him on the side of those who feel that rejecting the Church because of its weaknesses will not accomplish anything of lasting value. It will only lead to bitterness, hardness of heart, and blindness on the part of those who espouse this position. The result of all this is division — the aim of the evil one. I would rather exert my psychic energy toward acceptance of the weaknesses I see, knowing that they are my weaknesses too. I want to love the leaders in my church, knowing that love leads to clarity of vision and ultimately to unity of faith.

I do not aim at being conservative or liberal. I aim at discovering the truth in all its dimensions. The truth is not discovered by defensively trying to stop the clock or by being afraid of the future. It is discovered by living deeply in Jesus, who is the Truth, and by being open to and listening to the truth of the Spirit of Jesus.

We need leaders who courageously and compassionately embrace the follies and factions of a world that is drowning in its own sinful misery. But that same world is, at base, hungering for goodness and truth and will respond healthily, I believe, to leaders who have acknowledged their own weaknesses and point people to Jesus, the Good Shepherd.

As I take an honest look at the Church of today, I am not optimistic about the present or future. But I *am* hopeful. The present crisis is an opportunity to make a clear choice. I am betting that most people will come down on the side of faith (which is the opposite of fear) and continue to hope in a church that seeks the truth with the courage and compassion of Jesus.

~ *The truth is discovered by living deeply in Jesus, who is the Truth.*

~ 37 ~

Treasures of the Church

There's a story in the life of St. Lawrence, a deacon-martyr of the third century, that touches me deeply. In his great concern for justice and charity, Lawrence had given many of the treasures of the Church to the poor. The Roman prefect was furious and demanded that Lawrence return the treasures within four days. It took Lawrence all of four days to round up all the poor, the lame, the blind, and the leprous of Rome. To the Roman prefect he said: "Here, sir, are the treasures of the Church."

A real eye-opener, that! As long as the Church continues to lose sight of its primary mission of living and preaching the Gospel, it will fail to bring the life to people that Jesus came to give. Only a vibrant relationship with Jesus, and a constantly growing faith in Him, will keep the Church on course and bring healing to a languishing people.

Perhaps the healing that is most needed is the ever-recurring abuse of authority from top to bottom. Mostly at the top is this painfully evident. It is very difficult at times to see the living Gospel in those for whom power means nothing but domination. The only kind of power that Jesus speaks about is the spiritual power that has its origin in serving others, in seeking the last place. Jesus makes it very clear that only the childlike even know that the Kingdom of God exists. For the rest — for those whose hearts are engaged in the power struggle at all times — the Gospel remains a heady document full of beautiful words that cannot be realized in human affairs. Morris West said some time ago: "What authority forgets is that without the people who are the church, the hierarchy have voices talking to emptiness."

It is so refreshing to meet a humble cleric, perhaps because they are so few in number and so utterly disarming. One gets used to the cleric who stands on a pedestal calling for obeisance. Power does indeed corrupt the human heart, in a way and to a degree that nothing else does. And religion is an excellent backdrop from which to brow-beat people.

The anawim, the little people who are worthless in the eyes of the worldly wise, are the ones that put the proud to shame. Out of their honesty comes wisdom. From the simple heart flows more Gospel power than what flows from a million hearts that are cluttered with self. They are the treasures of the Church. It behooves us to listen to them.

~ *The only kind of power that Jesus speaks about is the spiritual power that has its origin in serving others, in seeking the last place.*

~ 38 ~

Count Your Blessings

It's raining today. My attitude toward the rain will determine what kind of a day it will be for me.

I can stand at the window and feel sorry for myself as I watch the raindrops trickle down the window-pane. I can bemoan the fact that I can't do the things that I wanted or planned to do outdoors. I can allow my spirit to droop with the daisies and drain away the energy that could be channeled in constructive ways. In a word, I can allow myself to be enslaved by what is happening outside me. I can live my life reacting to what I have no control over and can do nothing about. The focus is on *me*.

A healthier stance would be to accept what is and see the rain as a rich blessing. St. Francis was so in love and united with creation that he addressed all creatures as his brothers and sisters. He had as much reverence for an earthworm as he had for the pope. He especially loved Sister Water, "so useful and humble, precious and chaste." How could we live without water? How could this planet survive without rain, without the lakes and rivers and streams and all living things in the waters? How could we cook or keep ourselves clean without water? How would anything grow in fields to nourish our bodies without water?

Thomas Merton, shortly before his death in 1968, said something profoundly simple: "In joy, everything just as it is, whether 'for' or 'against': in peace, in universal acceptance, in Christ." As I get older, his words make more and more sense to me. It is that stance of a poor pilgrim in this world that will bring me happiness and peace. The more I cling to anything in this passing world, the more unhappy I will be for fear of losing it. I have been purchased by Christ at a great price, and I need to surrender all to him again and again. The life I live is not my own; it is *Christ* who lives in me. I must let go. I must accept all things just as they are. That is the healthy (and therefore holy) stance that brings freedom, love, and peace.

Thank God for the rain. Thank God for the precious gift of Sister Water. The focus is on *God* — where it should be.

~ *"In joy, everything just as it is, whether 'for' or 'against': in peace, in universal acceptance, in Christ."*
—Thomas Merton

~ 39 ~

Balance

There's a plant in my office that is very old. I've carried it with me for years now, whenever I've been asked to pull up anchor and head for another port.

It's a beautiful plant in a not-so-beautiful pot. I don't even know its name. That doesn't seem to matter. What matters is that it's still growing despite its age. Not quickly. *Never* quickly. Very slowly. When another leaf begins to appear, it takes at least a month before it's finally unfurled. But what excitement it holds as it slowly unfolds and at last faces fully the light of another day.

I keep turning it around to another position every few days. That way the leaves, each of them of many shades of fresh green, stay pyramidal on all sides. The plant keeps its balance and is beautiful from any view you take of it.

Our life is something like that. It must be exciting to God to see our "I've-got-a-secret" anticipation of tomorrow — despite our age, still growing, still reaching out to the Sun of Justice, slowly and imperceptibly at times because of life's hurts along the way. The next facet of our life that needs attention is arranged in such a way that both what was and what will be are distinct from what is — but at the same time intimately a part of both. Always he looks for balance — between the inside and the outside, and between the inward thrust and the outward thrust.

But the analogy breaks down when we think of the namelessness of that plant. There is no such thing in God's garden. He calls each of us by name. And every time he calls out our name we grow another inch. We come home to ourselves. We rest in the beauty that he has made, which is the Beauty that he is.

I've decided to give my plant a name. You will hear that name only in silence. If you hear it, let me know. For you and I will have heard the voice of God.

~ *He calls each of us by name. And every time he calls out our name we grow another inch. We come home to ourselves. We rest in the beauty that he has made, which is the Beauty that he is.*

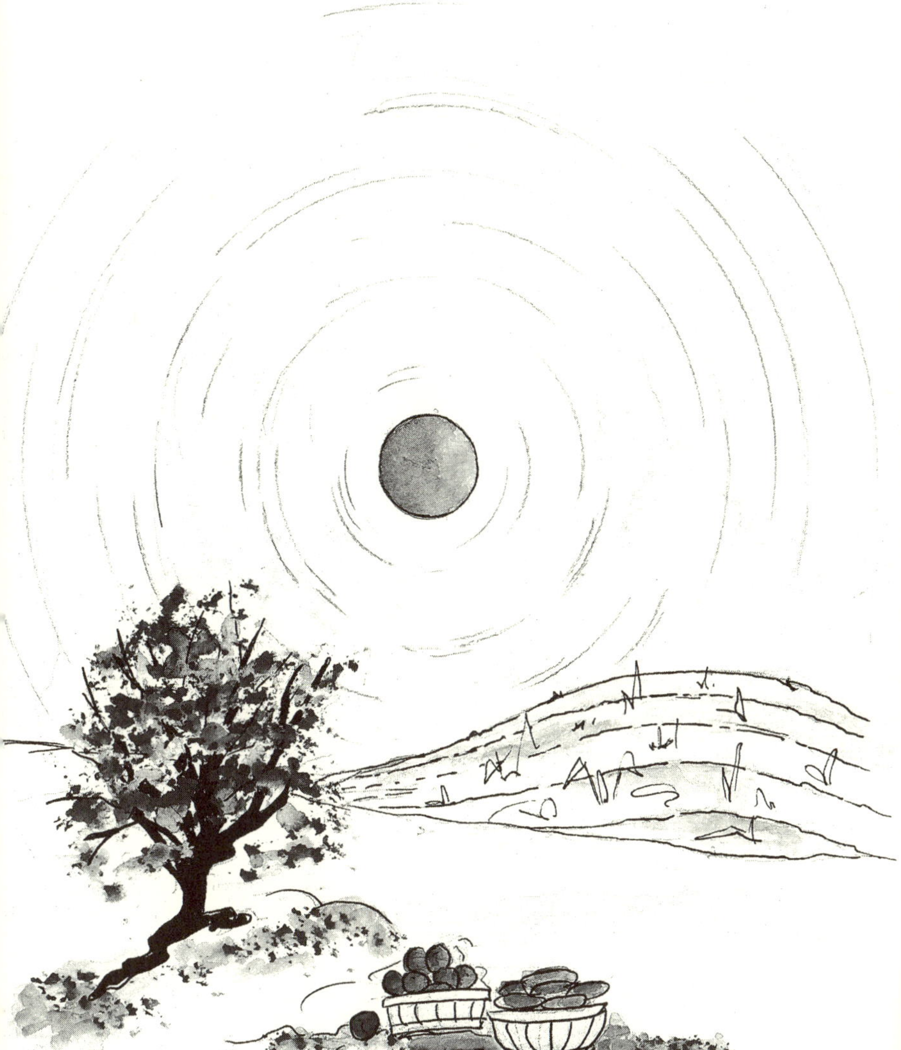

~ 40 ~

The New Jerusalem

I FIRST SAW "the new Jerusalem coming down out of heaven from God" (Rev 21) in the fall of 1969. I had just completed ten years of teaching at our high school-seminary, Mt. St. Francis, in southern Indiana, and I felt the Lord was leading me into some pastoral ministry. My soul was starved to experience what it meant to companion people in their journey of faith, only a bit of which I had tasted during my teaching years, mostly on weekend ministry in various parishes in the Louisville area. In God's providence, I was sent to be chaplain at St. Lawrence Hospital in Lansing, Michigan.

My stay there was enormously refreshing spiritually and was to last two years. Those two years were tumultuous in many ways. I was beginning to experience a mid-life crisis at age 40, which brought many headaches and heartaches that are still a mystery to me. But at the same time I was experiencing the real and personal love that God had for me in ways that defy words.

One of the most profound and lasting experiences began one night when I wandered into the room of a newly admitted patient and knew immediately that I was in the presence of a very holy person. He was a little old black man who was a Baptist minister of a church in Lansing. Though I learned from the nurses that he was dying, there was a radiant smile on his face that lit up the dark room that night and every night thereafter. I sat down beside him and held his hand, tasting the sweetness of the Lord. We just sat in silence for about ten minutes, both of us aware of the powerful presence of the Lord, and finally prayed the Our Father together. As I got up to leave, my friend whispered, "I see the new Jerusalem coming down out of heaven from God." I "saw" it with him with the eyes of faith. I left his room, awed by the mercy of God who had revealed himself to this man, and to me through him. I wanted to take off my shoes, for I stood on holy ground. Leaving his room, I went to the darkened chapel and just sat alone in God's presence in silence. There was nothing to say, nothing that needed to be said, and nothing that could be said, in that hour.

Each night for the next two weeks, after visiting the other patients, I spent my last ten minutes of ministry to the patients with my new friend. Always it was the same: the dimly lit room, the silence, the radiance of his face, the sparkle in his eyes, holding his hand, the Our Father, the new Jerusalem.

Finally my friend died. Or rather, he was taken up into the new Jerusalem. I felt sad in losing my dear friend. I knew very little *about* him, but I knew him deeply. We were bonded together for all eternity. That made the sting of his passing tolerable.

After all these years I still experience the radiant presence of my friend, especially in my priestly ministry. He has become one of my favorite saints. I wish I could remember his name. But then, I don't suppose it matters much.

~ *As I got up to leave, my friend whispered, "I see the new Jerusalem coming down out of heaven from God." I "saw" it with him with the eyes of faith.*

~ 41 ~

Intimacy

ALL OF US have intimacy needs which *must* be met. We all need to experience some degree of intimacy with others, some kind of contact. Otherwise we are doomed to spend our lives in isolation and loneliness, which, to say the least, is unhealthy.

For some, intimacy is maintained through speech. A regular kind of communication, however superficial it may be, is enough to ward off debilitating isolation.

For others, intimacy is achieved through doing things together; for example, playing sports or indoor games, or going to movies.

For most people, however, a greater degree of intimacy is needed — a personal sharing of the human heart. Sometimes just one other person with whom we can share our real self and concerns is sufficient. Sometimes several people are necessary.

Beneath all of this is the innate desire to be connected with others to some degree. Ultimately, it is the desire to be connected with God, whether we are willing to admit that or not.

The more deeply we long for intimacy with God and the more that longing is satisfied, the more capable we are of leading a spiritually healthy life. To be connected with God is to be connected with ourselves. It is to learn the fundamental truth that we gain our real identity from losing ourselves in God.

Until that happens in our life, we spend useless and exhausting time in search of ourselves by latching on to endless ways of drawing attention to ourselves in the hope of deceiving others into thinking that we have found ourselves. But of course we are only deceiving ourselves.

Those who have allowed themselves to be vulnerable, and thus transparent, are capable of the deepest kind of intimacy with others because they have learned to be intimate with themselves. There is no need anymore to put on a mask, to hide who they really are. They can face life confidently and comfortably because they have accepted their own imperfections and limitations. They don't have to pretend that they are perfect, nor do they have to pretend that anyone or anything else is perfect. They can simply be themselves.

In the end, it is only those who have embraced and endured the pain of being themselves who can live intimately with God, with themselves, with others.

~ *Those who have allowed themselves to be vulnerable, and thus transparent, are capable of the deepest kind of intimacy with others because they have learned to be intimate with themselves.*

~ 42 ~

Clowning in Cincinnati

In 1983 I had the good fortune of making a three-month internship program in Franciscan Spiritual Direction. About half-way through the program, we had an afternoon session of getting in touch with our shadow, in the Jungian sense of that part of us that we are not fully in touch with, are afraid of, and are constantly repressing. In a waking dream, with soft, dreamy music in the background, we were to go back in reverie to where we were stationed at the time and just follow the lead of the Spirit.

Accordingly, I went back in spirit to our Franciscan Retreat Center in Prior Lake, Minnesota. I passed the community room and saw that it was filled with Franciscan men from all over the Minneapolis-St. Paul area. They were all dressed in their Franciscan habits. I went to my room, just past the community room, and started to put on my habit to join the group meeting. Suddenly I decided not to put on my habit. I opened the closet door; and, to my surprise, there was a clown-suit hanging there. I put it on and skipped merrily into the community room, going around to each of the friars in greeting. One of the friars who lived with me at the retreat house said: "Kieran, stop your nonsense. Be yourself." I didn't seem to mind this criticism; I continued to enjoy myself with each of the friars, knowing in my depths that it was the right thing to do. At that point, I "awoke."

As I looked back on that experience, I realized that something significant had happened inside me: I got in touch with the shadowy part of myself — the clown within — that I had never touched before. That I — a quiet, reserved, introspective person all my life could have a clown hidden inside me was an incredible revelation. Others, in seeing or hearing about this experience, were drawn to say "Uh huh!" and encouraged me to let my clown emerge.

During the last ten years, I have done just that — letting my clown emerge. In the beginning, I felt very awkward, and I fell on my face very often. That was painful. But gradually, through those ten years, I have befriended my clown and let him emerge in a natural way whenever it felt right.

There are some important lessons that I have learned through all this:

1) A wholistic spiritual life cannot be established unless we embrace *all* of ourselves — the good and the bad. The shadowy part of ourselves must be allowed to emerge if we are to be made healthy and whole.

2) We are called by God to be grapes, not marbles. We are called to touch each other, not to keep each other at a distance. The more we allow ourselves to be vulnerable and broken (which all of us really are), the more Christ can bond us together and the more we learn, in our resultant transparency, what real intimacy is all about.

3) Being able to laugh at our own incongruities, inconsistencies, and foolishness is a marvelous way of opening ourselves up to an incarnational enjoyment of life in all its facets. It releases us to be who we really are, which is the only person that God can deal with.

4) This whole process of unmasking ourselves — or rather of allowing ourselves to be unmasked — is the work of God, from beginning to end. All we can do is let it happen. And even our desire to let it happen is God's work. It's a humbling experience; that is, it's a refreshing plunge into Truth.

Clowns, I have come to see, are beautiful people. And powerful people. We need to respect them. They can teach us a great deal about life. Which is what Jesus, the consummate Clown, has come to give us.

~ 43 ~

A Temple for God

Not long ago, Bishop James Malone of Youngstown, Ohio, came to Sancta Clara Monastery (home of our Poor Clare Sisters) in Canton, to bless our newly renovated church. It was a festive occasion, full of the kind of splendor that is good for the people of God to see. Ritual that is sensitively done — not drawing attention to itself, but leading people to a blend of the transcendence and immanence of God — can be marvelously uplifting. This ceremony was uplifting.

Before the ceremony began, Bishop Malone mingled with the people in church, as is his custom. In his own unique way, he became a model for that kind of blend of transcendence and immanence. Without saying it, he made it clear to the people that *they* are the church; and that as their visible shepherd, his delightful responsibility was to try to make Christ present to them. The people obviously loved him for his pastoral care. He was both for them and with them.

The ceremony became a catalyst for the profound truth that *we* are the living temples of God. Paul says it so powerfully: "You are strangers and aliens no longer. No, you are fellow citizens of the saints and members of the household of God. You form a building which rises on the foundation of the apostles and prophets, with Christ Jesus himself as the capstone. Through him the whole structure is fitted together and takes shape as a holy temple in the Lord; in him you are being built into this temple, to become a dwelling place for God in the Spirit" (Eph 2:19–22).

Hence the reverence that we need to have for each other. Jesus, in the Incarnation, has made it abundantly clear that humanity is an excellent conductor of divinity. As people made in the image of God and as dwelling places for God, we need to take off our shoes in each other's presence. We need to bow to each other. And we need to bow before the beauty of all creation, which is meant to be a diaphanous revelation of God's goodness and mercy, power and glory.

In this age of throw-aways, which is riddled with a flippancy toward everything that we hold sacred, we need to remember this vision of ourselves and the universe. If we don't, we open ourselves to a continuing spiral downward into crime from which there is no return. A massive buildup of police on the beat may turn up the heat; but unless there is a return to sanity based on the proper vision of God and man, we will continue to flounder. A spiritual problem demands a spiritual solution.

Only when each of us, plumbing the depth of who we are before God and seeing our own uniqueness, can reverence ourselves as *living* stones in the temple that God is building, will we be able to enter the human scene with the kind of power that comes from God. And the only kind of power that God gives us is the power to see clearly and value infinitely another human being and all of creation as worthy of our reverence.

A dear friend, who understands all this and has the courage and power from God to live this out in her daily walk of faith, recently gave me cause to pause when she said: "I played my drum For Him; I played my beat for Him; I played my drum for Him." That says it all.

> ~ *Jesus, in the Incarnation, has made it abundantly clear that humanity is an excellent conductor of divinity. As people made in the image of God and as dwelling places for God, we need to take off our shoes in each other's presence.*

~ 44 ~

All That Glitters

I DON'T PRAY for the conversion of Russia anymore; I pray for the conversion of America. I pray that our eyes may be opened to the truth about our own spiritual blindness. I pray that we may accept the challenge that we are presently faced with and not back off — the challenge to face our own superficiality, our own preoccupation with how we *appear* in the eyes of the world. How we appear is really not important; how we *are* is terribly important.

What we as a nation need is a massive dose of humility, enabling us to lay aside the illusions that we are caught up in. No longer can we afford, if ever we could, to attack the enemy "out there," to project our deficiencies on an enemy that isn't the real enemy at all. We must face the fact that we have been our own worst enemy. We need, in a word, to own our sinfulness.

We are, I believe, in the grips of a national — indeed, a global — dark night of the soul. All the glitter that the world offers and that we glibly ran after in the fat yesteryears is now seen for what it really is: glitter without substance or substantial significance. *Sic transit gloria mundi.*

The challenge that now lies before us is to re-examine our priorities and choose a more human and humane response to life, a more loving and compassionate way of living. We need to stay with the darkness inside, feel the pain that is a necessary concomitant to God's stripping love, and allow the transformation from within to happen. We need to let go of all the trifles we cling to so that our vision of what is right and good may emerge. I like what William McNamara says, "Because we are not at home in dark deep faith, in the Stygian stages of life, led by divine life alone, we go for any flash of light, however spurious; and so we are committed to egregious folly."

This could be our finest hour, but only if we choose wisely and well. It could also be our most abysmal hour, from which we may never recover.

The choice is ours. I pray that we may come down on the side of what is right, not what is expedient.

~ *"Because we are not at home in dark deep faith, in the Stygian stages of life, led by divine life alone, we go for any flash of light, however spurious; and so we are committed to egregious folly."*
—William McNamara

~ 45 ~

What's in a Fad?

ONE OF THE WAYS in which we can judge the substance of a culture is to check on its slavery to, or freedom from, fads. All people are enslaved to some extent by fads. Unfortunately, that is to be expected in a cellophane age. I speak here, however, about *most* people on what passes for the American scene.

I find the overwhelming majority of Americans preoccupied with image — how they appear, how they come across, how they are perceived. All of this is the result of gross insecurity. It matters not to people who they are and what they are meant to be, as derived from an inner Source of Strength; all that matters is that they appear to be relevant, as derived from some arbitrary source of acceptability.

That state of affairs is terribly sad to me. It says to me that there is a lamentable lack of interiority out of which the godly can emanate. And if that is the case, then I must use all manner of means to hide the shallowness that, in my sobering moments, I *know* is the real me. But because I have neither the courage nor the stamina to face my hollowness, I continue to babble on with words, words, words as a cover-up.

Sooner or later I will be challenged by someone who is not fooled by my phoney exterior and who loves me enough to risk removing my mask. I will be forced to face the truth about myself. That is my hallowed moment of grace, when I must choose to live or die. If I choose to live, then I must resist the values of a world that has always been, and will always be, at enmity with Truth. I must let go of all the externals that I have used in an attempt to be relevant. I must dare to risk being my real self. And paradoxically, that life-long process can only commence and continue as I am willing to die to the images of myself that I have constructed through years of self-deceit. The way to life, then, is through death to my false self. Lose yourself in me, Jesus said, and you will find yourself.

If I choose to die the death of stagnation, I must then expend all of my self-defeating energy to continue the charade. In that case, I am choosing to bury the real me in layer after layer of externals that may make me acceptable to others of the same persuasion, but confine me to the dark regions of inner meaninglessness and obscurity.

Choose life. Choose to come out from hiding. Breathe the fresh air of freedom. Seek Him who alone can free you from your captivity of living up to the expectations of others. The only expectations that you need to live up to are God's. And all He asks is that, by his grace, you allow the beautifully unique you to break through the rich soil of freedom. That freedom belongs only to the children of God.

~ *There is a lamentable lack of interiority out of which the godly can emanate.*

~ *The only expectations that you need to live up to are God's.*

~ 46 ~

To Be a Saint

WE BURIED our Franciscan Brother Francis this morning. He was 67. That he was 67 doesn't seem to matter much; it seems like an unnecessary and peripheral bit of information, not only for Francis, but for anyone who has died. It just seems to be expected to tell a person's age when he dies, that's all. (Forgive me the sexist language; I use "he/him" from now on only because it is less clumsy.)

I'm going to make a statement about Francis that I've never made in exactly the same way about anyone else in my life's experience: Francis, I think, was a saint.

I have often heard it said about a person after death, "He wasn't a saint, but...." That statement always sounded hollow to me — hollow and distracting, as if a saint were a person who was perfect and didn't have the imperfections and peccadillos that the rest of us mortals have. That is not my understanding of what a saint is.

A saint, to my way of thinking (and I'm using Brother Francis now as a model), is a person who believes deeply in the mercy and compassion of God in spite of, or perhaps because of, his sinfulness. He believes so deeply in God's mercy that he is totally focused on it and will not allow himself to be in any way preoccupied with, or discouraged by, his sinfulness, even though he is always aware of that in the subconscious. I am convinced that that is the way God views the situation, and that that is the only way we as saved sinners can healthily live. Our sinfulness can only be rightly seen against the backdrop of God's infinite and unconditional love and mercy.

A saint is, further, a person who knows who he is by reason of his immersion in Christ. He is rooted in Christ; which is to say, he has found his identity in Christ from having died with Him in baptism and has experienced the truth of the Paschal Mystery in his life. He has, in a word, shed his ego, allowing that false, inflated self to die by the transforming power of God, so that his real self may emerge. He has allowed his real self to be found by God by dying to that part of himself which clamors for center-stage.

This kind of transformation does not ordinarily happen in a moment. It seems God looks to the long haul, and helps us to come into the truth little by little, over the course of many years of being broken open by many "failures" (as the wisdom of the world would measure success and failure).

A saint, then, is not driven to act according to what others expect of him, but according to the inner vision that he has gained from losing himself in God. He is not swayed by conventional wisdom which says that image is important and that image must be maintained at all costs. He does not care that he is, or is not, *au courant*. The only thing that drives him is what *God* expects of him, now and in this situation of life.

I loved Brother Francis. I thank him for leaving me a rich legacy of what I think it means to be a saint. The only way that I can honor him satisfactorily and acceptably is by trying, as he did, to embrace *all* of myself (the good and the not-so-good), and to continue to seek God and his will passionately, with every breath that I draw. I need to remember always that Jesus is my friend and desires intimate union with me infinitely more than I could ever ask or imagine. And that fills my heart with joy and gratitude.

~ *A saint, then, is not driven to act according to what others expect of him, but according to the inner vision that he has gained from losing himself in God.*

~ 47 ~

Wells for Others

MY FRIEND JOHN went home to the Father today. For the last eight years he suffered interminably with a terminal cancer of the bones. He was largely confined to bed during the past year.

John had an irrepressible desire for life — which is to say, he had an insatiable desire for Jesus, who is Life. In all the times I visited him, I cannot recall his ever complaining about his sickness. Always he had a smile. Always he was centered on Jesus, who, he felt, showed him immense love by inviting him into the intimacy of redemptive suffering. John was fully aware of all the suffering in the world, and he was fully aware of all the useless suffering that people bring on themselves as the result of foolishness and sin. It would not be that way with John.

Someone has said that when loss has become freedom, we are baptized with wonder and are fit to die. As John's body disintegrated before our very eyes, his spirit took on light and radiance. His eyes became bright with the wonder and excitement of a child who has been gifted with a new toy. Loss had been transformed into the freedom to be God's child. There was nothing to be afraid of, nothing to defend, nothing to store in barns. He allowed himself to be stripped of everything and, in return, he was given all that was of real value — joy and peace and a loving spirit to accept life as it was.

Because of John's intimacy with Jesus through pain and suffering, he became a well for people to come and drink from. The well of eternal life was forever springing up within

John, as Jesus said it would. That's where John's strength came from, and that's where the strength came from that others experienced in visiting John. His spirit proclaimed a hearty welcome to all who came to him. They left him, knowing that they had touched Jesus the Well, to whom John always pointed people.

What a different world we would have if all of us became wells for people to drink from. That takes a security that is born of God. All our trust is in him who is Life, outside of whom there are only shadows and illusions. All our addictions and compulsions that are born of a small and self-centered world fall away. We are free at last, as John was, to revel in the freedom and glory of being children of God. We see at last that our losses are really gains, and we are fit to die long before God calls us to himself. The letting go has led us home to God, in whom we rest secure, now and forever.

The words of St. Teresa come to mind: "Let nothing disturb you, nothing frighten you. All things are passing. God alone suffices." For John, God was enough. For all of us, God can be enough.

~ *What a different world we would have if all of us became wells for people to drink from.*

~ *"Let nothing disturb you, nothing frighten you. All things are passing. God alone suffices."*
—St. Teresa

~ 48 ~

Sacred Relationships

I FIND MYSELF longing for more and more solitude lately. Not because I am less fond of people, but because relationships are becoming more and more sacred to me.

My relationship with *God* has taken on new color and excitement as I allow him to become the center of my life. My thoughts are more focused on him and less on myself — my own private little wars, my plans, my hurts, my ambitions, my addictions — and in the process I find that I am entering the arena of life with more eagerness to live fully. I can take off my armor and stand more vulnerably before my God and let him have his way with me, trusting that all the experiences of my life this day — whether they bring me joy or pain — are a gift of a loving and compassionate God who does nothing amiss. He is a source of such joy to me that I want to give him all the time he needs to lift me from the morass of my own tenuousness and ease me into the encircling arms of his monumental strength. As a consequence, my prayer time encompasses the whole day, not just a small portion of it. My Friend deserves that.

My relationship with *myself* has become more easeful, less strained. I seek to be alone, no longer to retreat from life's hurts, but to be with a Presence that is life-giving and nourishing. I am more comfortable with myself, more accepting of myself as I am, with all my brokenness and sinfulness and dis-ease. My limitations have become a source of grace and blessing to me because through them the power of a loving God can be proclaimed and manifested. I reverence myself and take off my shoes more because I am more delicately attuned to him who lives within me, who speaks to me the words of eternal life. I believe in myself, my own importance, my place in the universe.

My relationship with *others* is enriching because the time alone has been so rich. There are sparks in the sharing because solitude has become togetherness in a real sense. Even the silence with others is nourishing and uplifting. Peace has become not the mere absence of war, but the reinforcement of an acceptance of life as it is.

It's amazing to me that people will resort to all sorts of demonic attempts to avoid being alone. And so the noise pollution intensifies, and the incessant chatter about "sweet nothings" fills all the cracks of life. But off in some lonely part of the world, one person — seemingly small and insignificant to the sophisticated — holds the world together because he is together and knows a peace that surpasses all understanding. Thank God for that person. *It could be you.*

I like what Douglas Steere says in *Together in Solitude:* "There is no task God has called us to that is more exciting and challenging than being made inwardly ready to be present where we are."

> ~ *I find myself longing for more and more solitude lately. Not because I am less fond of people, but because relationships are becoming more and more sacred to me.*

~ 49 ~

The Resurgence of Women

I THANK GOD for making me the way I am. The feminine part of me (the anima that Jung speaks about) is fairly well developed. For that, I have not only God to thank, but also my mother, my sisters, the Dominican Sisters who taught me in grade school, and the many women whom I have befriended in my thirty-nine years of priestly ministry. I am especially grateful for the last twenty years of ministry in spiritual direction and directed retreats. For the most part, the people that I have companioned during these years have been women. They have taught me a great deal about what it means to be a man after the heart of Jesus. They have drawn out of me what lay hidden for many years of my childhood, but especially during my adolescence.

As far back as I can remember, I felt out of step with most of the rest of my gender. I felt uneasy with those whose consuming interest seemed to be in developing a macho image. I was repulsed by those who wanted to prove their power by bullying others into submission. Gradually I came to see that my understanding of what it meant to be a whole man was nothing to be ashamed of; on the contrary, it was a gift to be cherished. What I prized in a man was sensitivity, understanding, honesty, and compassion. In clerical circles, I found precious few men who were not consumed by what Maggie Ross calls the seven P's: power, pretension, presumption, pomposity, privilege, preferment, and patronage. I looked to Jesus and found none of these — only prayerfulness and pastoral care. I looked to Francis and he pointed me back to Jesus.

As I listened to the Gospel, I saw how comfortable Jesus was with women, and they with him. They understood each other and accepted each other as complementary, and so learned the meaning of life by being brothers and sisters to each other. Women were the last to be with Jesus in his death, and the first to announce his resurrection. I began to see why Jesus might not have chosen women to be his inner circle of companions: they already knew divinity because of their understanding of birthing and suffering, compassion and sacrifice. Jesus may have chosen men because they did not innately know these things. They had to be taught them over and over again. Jesus had to put a child in their midst to remind them what the kingdom was all about. Their preoccupation with the seven P's had to be dealt with so that they could learn how to climb *down* the ladder and put on aprons and wash feet. These were things that women already knew.

Jesus calls *all* of us to be his mothers: "Whoever does the will of God is my brother and sister and mother" (Mk 3:35). To think that celebrating the Incarnation in a priestly way is the exclusive right of men is a "scandal."* Men need to ponder the humility of God — Jesus *emptied* himself (Phil 2:7) — and submit ourselves to the painful process of metanoia to learn what our sisters have known from the beginning. Until that time, we can only pray that our sisters will continue to be patient with the birthing process and the painful kicking that we men need to experience in order to come forth from the womb of God.

> ~ *As I listened to the Gospel, I saw how comfortable Jesus was with women, and they with him. They understood each other and accepted each other as complementary, and so learned the meaning of life by being brothers and sisters to each other.*

---

*Cf. the editorial of Dan Turner, *Creation Spirituality,* Nov.–Dec., 1993.

~ 50 ~

The Gift of Depression

NONE OF US *like* to be sad, melancholic, depressed. If we did, we would be very sick and would need therapeutic attention. We all would like to be happy all the time. But we know from experience that depression is a fact of life; and the more we try to avoid it, the more we shall experience it. Jesus said, in so many words, that the more we run from the cross, the more we shall experience the pain of it. Conversely, the more we embrace the cross that is built into life, the more we shall experience the fullness of life which Jesus has come to give. We come at last to see that the only way *out of* depression is *through* it.

During most of 1987, I fell into a deep depression. I spent most of that year in such a depressed state that it took every ounce of strength in me to put one foot in front of the other. I wandered in the desert of New Mexico, walking miles and miles with sand in my mouth, feeling worthless, alone, and helpless. It was the most painful experience of my life; and every night before retiring, I prayed that the Lord would take me while I slept so that I would not have to face the pain of another day. When I awakened in the morning, I became more deeply depressed. There was simply no light at the end of the tunnel. For most of that year, I constantly struggled with ways in which I might end my life. There was no real color left; I could only see black and grey.

The reasons for the depression were many and varied. But in the end, they did not matter much. What I needed to do, I found, was to embrace the pain, feel it in the depths of who I was, and let it be. Like the farmer who plants his seed in the earth and then trusts that it will germinate and produce fruit in due time (Jas 5:7), I had to believe that what was happening deep within me was what I needed; that, in spite of my sinfulness, or rather because of it, God loved me and his love for me neither could nor would change; that all of the pain was for a reason which I could not understand at the time and perhaps would never understand; and that I needed to be patient with what was happening, trusting that God in his way and in his time would use this experience to transform me into a better person and a better channel for his grace to flow unobstructedly.

As I look back on that year, I see it as the gift that it really was. Gibran says that the deeper the pain is carved into our being, the more capacity there is for joy. That, I think, is profoundly true. I am constantly aware of the depths of depression that I experienced, and so I am infinitely more sensitive to the slightest and most obscure evidence of joy in life. I am much more in tune with the suffering of others because of my own pain, and I am therefore more compassionate in the face of the suffering that others are enduring. And because God gave me the grace to embrace my pain and not run away from it, I am much more capable of intimacy with myself and therefore with others.

Depression, therefore, is not so much an illness to be cured; it is a gift from a loving God who knows all our ways and who wants us to live fully and joyfully each moment as it comes. And God, in his infinite wisdom, knows exactly the kind, the amount, and the intensity of pain that is needed for us to experience the kingdom of joy and love and peace.

There is a time for tears. And all we can say in the end is that even God knew that time of seeming abandonment, meaninglessness, and hopelessness, and in it he did not despair. Neither may we.

~ *We come at last to see that the only way* out of *depression is* through *it.*

~ 51 ~

Stillness

"**M**EASURE YOUR LOVE WITH STILLNESS," writes Jessica Powers (in "O Spirita Sancta"). What does stillness have to do with love? Everything!

Let us face it: we are poor lovers, and we always shall be. Just a glance at the morning paper, just a glimpse of the evening news will convince us of this if we need convincing. But those who are awake and at least somnolently perceptive do not need to go that far; they need only take a moment's notice inside themselves to see the chaos and the ravages of time.

Why are we so chaotic, tugged hither and yon by a world that is forested with traps that point us to happiness — and lo, we fall repeatedly into those traps? Because our heads keep swirling with words heard on the air-waves that beckon us to the thrills of a new toy. And we fall prey to that magnetic call of the wild that has only the merest semblance of truth. It is the call of the world that has always been at enmity with the harmoniously beautiful world of God's creating.

But beneath all of that — beneath the surface of our spongy minds — the problem rests with our restless hearts. The enemy is within us. We are not still enough to see the often-slight difference between love and unlove, between tough love and sentimental love, between the real thing and its semblance. "It is only with the heart that one sees rightly; what is essential is invisible to the eye," says the wise Little Prince. What is essential escapes us because only Love can awaken us to a clear understanding of reality. And Love can only heal our blindness when we are still, when we are receptive, when we have learned to rest at the fountain of Truth and Beauty within us.

"Love is not loved," Francis of Assisi used to cry out of the depths of his enlightened heart. Of course! How can we respond in love to a God who is Love — not to mention knowing him with any degree of accuracy — when our hearts are freighted and taut and strained with unstillness? "Love has its proper soil, its native land...love must out of Love begin," Powers says; and its proper soil is stillness.

~ *Love can awaken us to a clear understanding of reality. And Love can only heal our blindness when we are still, when we are receptive, when we have learned to rest at the fountain of Truth and Beauty within us.*

~ *"Love has its proper soil, its native land...love must out of Love begin."*

—Jessica Powers

~ 52 ~

A King Forever

LET US LISTEN DEEPLY to God's word through Paul (Col 1):
"He (God) brought us into the kingdom of his beloved Son.... He (Christ) is the image of the invisible God, the first-born of all creatures. In him everything in heaven and on earth was created, things visible and invisible. All were created through him; all were created for him. He is before all else that is. In him everything continues in being. It is he who is head of the body, the church! He who is the beginning, the first-born of the dead, so that primacy may be his in everything."

Let us pray to Christ our King:

Jesus, we acclaim and proclaim you as our King. But even as we say that — and we say it with our whole heart — we know that in our weakness we can betray you. Our mind can become dark and our will weak and we can fall in the face of trial. Our fall is inevitable if we rely on our own power which is no power at all. Make us remember, Jesus, that without you we are and can do nothing.

Give us the courage to allow you to turn the spotlight on our hearts, to search out all the dark areas of ourselves that are not wholly yours. Help us to see all the idols — power, prestige, honor, money — that we cling to even as we acclaim you as King. Give us the strength to let go of them, one by one, until we are left stripped of vacuous power and defenses.

Disarm us with your love, Jesus; assure us that even as we let go of all our pretensions of holiness, you love us still. Give us humility to face ourselves as we really are — not as we

think we are, and not as we want others to think we are —
and deliver us from pride, which is the heaviest of burdens.

Keep our focus on you, not on ourselves. And let us not be overwhelmed by our sinfulness, but allow you to save us from our foolishness and treachery.

Give us eyes to see your kingdom clearly wherever we find joy, justice, peace, love. Let your invisible kingdom be more real and demanding than the visible kingdoms of puppets and pariahs and profiteers. And bond us together with all our brothers and sisters, constantly looking beyond all the external differences that could be the source of division. Draw us together in love and compassion, that the world may believe in you and be led to the kind of surrender to you that you ask for and are worthy of.

Jesus, even as the kingdoms of the world are all passing away, hold us close to your heart in your kingdom that will endure forever. May we sing your praise and glory, now and always. Amen.

Also from Resurrection Press...

PRACTICING THE PRAYER OF PRESENCE (Revised Edition)
by Susan Muto and Adrian van Kaam

This book opens us to the peace and purpose of living a life of Christian prayer. It teaches us how to pray and especially how to appreciate and practice the prayer of presence.... Woven throughout the text are quotes and prayers that may inspire you to commit yourself to a new way of life, a way of prayer, that may prove to be as challenging as it is transforming."
— *From the Preface*

"...both inspiration and guide for men and women in their efforts to shape a contemplative life in the midst of busy demands and complex duties." — Dolores R. Leckey, Director
Secretariat for Family Life, Laity, Women, and Youth

"All who read and study this book will be permanently rewarded."
— Fr. Benedict Groeschel, C.F.R.

ISBN 1-878718-14-2 192pp. $7.95

A powerful sequel to the bestselling Miracle Hour

5-MINUTE MIRACLES
Praying for People with Simplicity and Power, by Linda Schubert

"A gift to the Church today.... Linda Schubert has undoubtedly birthed a second miracle! A must read for all who desire to comfort others by praying with them and for those who have not yet dared to desire."
— Babsie Bleasdell

"Not just a gem, but a treasure-trove of inspiration.... Linda Schubert demonstrates that arm-around-the-shoulder informality plus let's-pray-about-it compassion can draw five-minute miracles from a God of incandescent love." — John H. Hampsch, C.M.F.

LINDA SCHUBERT is the author of *Miracle Hour,* which has sold over 400,000 copies, and is a worldwide speaker on the power of prayer.

ISBN 1-878718-08-8 64pp. $3.95

Published by Resurrection Press

Discovering Your Light Margaret O'Brien	$6.95
The Gift of the Dove Joan M. Jones, PCPA	$3.95
Healing through the Mass Robert DeGrandis, SSJ	$7.95
His Healing Touch Michael Buckley	$7.95
Let's Talk James P. Lisante	$7.95
A Celebration of Life Anthony Padovano	$7.95
Miracle in the Marketplace Henry Libersat	$5.95
Give Them Shelter Michael Moran	$6.95
Heart Business Dolores Torrell	$6.95
A Path to Hope John Dillon	$5.95
The Healing of the Religious Life Faricy/Blackborow	$6.95
Transformed by Love Margaret Magdalen, CSMV	$5.95
RVC Liturgical Series: The Liturgy of the Hours	$3.95
The Lector's Ministry	$3.95
Behold the Man Judy Marley, SFO	$3.50
I Shall Be Raised Up	$2.25
From the Weaver's Loom Donald Hanson	$7.95
In the Power of the Spirit Kevin Ranaghan	$6.95
Young People and...You Know What William O'Malley	$3.50
Lights in the Darkness Ave Clark, O.P.	$8.95
Practicing the Prayer of Presence van Kaam/Muto	$7.95
5-Minute Miracles Linda Schubert	$3.95
Nothing but Love Robert Lauder	$3.95
Faith Means...If You Pray for Rain, Bring an Umbrella Antoinette Bosco	$3.50
Stress and the Search for Happiness van Kaam/Muto	$3.95
Harnessing Stress van Kaam/Muto	$3.95
Healthy and Holy under Stress van Kaam/Muto	$3.95

Spirit-Life Audiocassette Collection

Witnessing to Gospel Values Paul Surlis	$6.95
Celebrating the Vision of Vatican II Michael Himes	$6.95
Hail Virgin Mother Robert Lauder	$6.95
Praying on Your Feet Robert Lauder	$6.95
Annulment: Healing-Hope-New Life Thomas Molloy	$6.95
Life After Divorce Tom Hartman	$6.95
Path to Hope John Dillon	$6.95
Thank You Lord! McGuire/DeAngelis	$8.95
Spirit Songs Jerry DeAngelis	$9.95

Resurrection Press books and cassettes are available in your local religious bookstore. If you want to be on our mailing list for our up-to-date announcements, please write or phone:

Resurrection Press
P.O. Box 248, Williston Park, NY 11596
1-800-89 BOOKS